Dan Fouts
Ken Anderson
Joe Theismann
and Other All-Time **GREAT QUARTERBACKS**

Dan Fouts
Ken Anderson
Joe Theismann
and Other All-Time GREAT
QUARTERBACKS

illustrated with photographs

edited by Phyllis and Zander Hollander

A ZANDER HOLLANDER SPORTS BOOK

Random House New York

Library of Congress Cataloging in Publication Data:
Main entry under title:
Dan Fouts, Ken Anderson, Joe Theismann, and other all-time great quarterbacks.
  "A Zander Hollander sports book."
  SUMMARY: Profiles of ten football superstars: Joe Theismann, Ken Anderson, Roger Staubach, Dan Fouts, Joe Namath, Joe Montana, Terry Bradshaw, Bob Griese, Fran Tarkenton, and Johnny Unitas.   1. Quarterback (Football)—Biography—Juvenile literature. [1. Football players] I. Hollander, Phyllis. II. Hollander, Zander. III. Title.
GV939.A1D34   1983   796.332′092′2   [B]   [920]   83-4543
ISBN: 0-394-85805-0 (pbk.)

The photographs in this book appear courtesy of: Malcolm W. Emmons, pages 55, 91, 119; Richard Pilling, page 15; Carl Skalak, Jr., page 104; San Diego / Sports Photo Source, page 43; United Press International, pages 2, 13, 26, 62, 67, 81.

Manufactured in the United States of America
1 2 3 4 5 6 7 8 9 0

Acknowledgments

Without a strong supporting cast, even the finest quarterbacks are in for rough passage. In quarterbacking *Great Quarterbacks*, the editors were fortunate in having a team that helped them reach the end zone. They acknowledge with appreciation the contributions of writers Eric Compton of the New York *Daily News*, who wrote the chapter on Ken Anderson; David Kaplan (Roger Staubach); Dave Newhouse of the Oakland *Tribune* (Dan Fouts); Martin Lader of United Press International (Joe Namath and Terry Bradshaw); Frank Kelly of the New York *Daily News* (Joe Montana and Bob Griese); and Pete Alfano of *The New York Times* (Fran Tarkenton and Johnny Unitas). The chapter on Joe Theismann was written by Zander Hollander.

Contents

Introduction

He calls the signals and leads the team. He gets the most headlines and the most trophies. When his team wins, he gets the cheers; when his team loses, he gets the boos.

He is the quarterback.

Whether he's playing in the Pop Warner League, high school, college, or the National Football League, the quarterback has to keep his cool while the big pass-rushers zoom in on him like missiles. At the last second before his feet are knocked out from under him, he has to fire the ball at a receiver's ear.

He has the most important and most glamorous job in football. That's why most young football players want to be quarterbacks.

There is no secret formula for becoming a quarterback. But it's vital to have a good arm, a good head, and the ability to take punishment. All three qualities propelled the super-quarterbacks in this book into successful careers in the NFL. But each had his own special path to stardom.

Great Quarterbacks includes 10 of the greatest modern quarterbacks—a mixture of active players in the 1980s and stars of the recent past whose achievements have made them legendary figures.

—Phyllis and Zander Hollander

Dan Fouts
Ken Anderson
Joe Theismann
and Other All-Time **GREAT**
QUARTERBACKS

JOE THEISMANN
Voice of the Redskins

It was late in the third period of Super Bowl XVII on January 30, 1983. The Miami Dolphins were leading the Washington Redskins, 17–13, before a crowd of 103,677 at the Rose Bowl in Pasadena, California. More than 100,000,000 fans were watching on NBC television, and all eyes were on Redskin quarterback Joe Theismann as he took the snap from center on the Washington 17-yard line.

Theismann dropped back near the goal line and threw a pass to Charlie Brown, but Miami's 6-foot-6 Kim Bokamper tipped the ball. All Bokamper had to do was to catch it and run three yards for a touchdown. But Theismann, diving like a cornerback, reached from behind the Miami defensive end and knocked the ball away to save the interception.

An alert Joe Theismann (7) lunges just in time to knock the ball out of the hands of Miami's Kim Bokamper in the third quarter of Super Bowl XVII.

It was the defensive play of the game, but Washington still trailed by four points. With 10 minutes remaining in the game and the Redskins determined to mount a scoring drive, Theismann handed off to fullback John Riggins on the Miami 43. Riggins, known as The Diesel for his locomotive power, cut left, shook off Miami cornerback Don McNeal, and raced 43 yards down the sideline for a touchdown.

Ahead for the first time, Washington scored another touchdown on a Theismann pass to Brown—and suddenly it was all over. The Redskins had beaten the Dolphins, 27–17, and were Super Bowl champions for the first time.

Riggins was voted the Most Valuable Player for his record-breaking 168 yards, 38 carries, and game-winning touchdown. But the Redskins couldn't have done it without Theismann, who connected on 15 of 23 passes, including two touchdowns, and picked up 20 yards on three carries.

"I can't believe it, I can't believe it," Theismann kept repeating in the locker room. "This is everything I've always wanted."

As a 17-year-old in South River, New Jersey, Joe had watched the first Super Bowl on television in 1967 when the Green Bay Packers walloped the Kansas City Chiefs, 35–10. As the star quarterback at South River High School, he daydreamed then of playing in the Super Bowl. Now his dream had come true.

It was a dream that his grandpa Joe Theismann couldn't have had. Grandpa had come to the United States from Austria-Hungary in 1913 and settled on a farm in Bucks County, Pennsylvania, where he raised chickens. Joe's dad (also named Joe) was born there and moved to South River, where the Redskins' Joe was born on September 9, 1949.

Joey, as he was called, played ball in his early days in the lot next door to the Theismann home. "Whatever bounced, he played," noted his grandfather.

Joe started throwing a football through a tire he'd hung on a post. He would begin close to the tire, and every time he tossed the ball through the hole, he'd move back a couple of feet. He was on the way to becoming a quarterback.

But Joey's mother wouldn't let him play tackle football until he was 12 years old. "I didn't weigh very much and she was afraid I'd get hurt," he said.

Joe played basketball, Little League baseball, and then Pop Warner League football. By the time he got to South River High, he was recognized as a fine all-around athlete.

He made the varsity in all three sports but missed most of his junior year of football due to an injury—not from football. While swimming with his friends one summer day, he dove into shallow water and dislocated his shoulder. His father breathed a sigh of relief when he learned it was Joe's left shoulder and not his throwing arm. Even so, Joe would need surgery.

Joe had the operation in the summer of 1965 and was fully recovered when he started his senior year. And what a year it was! The 5-foot-10, 148-pound quarterback threw 23 touchdown passes to lead the team to an unbeaten season. Joe's favorite target in football was Drew Pearson, who would one day become a star receiver with the Dallas Cowboys.

Joe was also an all-state shortstop in baseball (a .300 hitter and an excellent fielder) and an all-county guard in basketball.

As graduation day approached, Joe had to decide which college to attend. His high-school coach, Ron Wojcicki, was a graduate of North Carolina State and Joe almost went there. But two visits to the campus at Notre Dame convinced him that that was the place to be—for a fine education as well as for football.

He settled on Notre Dame despite the fact

that a writer on a New Jersey newspaper warned that as a 148-pounder he would be "killed" if he tried to play at a big-time college like Notre Dame. The day he walked onto the freshman practice field, coach Johnny Ray shook his head and said, "What's this skinny kid doing here? These big guys will murder him."

As a freshman Joe soon discovered he'd made the right decision. He was elected captain of the freshman team. With 40 seconds to go in the only game it played, against Pittsburgh, he threw his third touchdown pass to bring the Irish a 21–18 victory. And he didn't get killed.

Dating back to his earliest days of competitive football, Joe was the picture of confidence. Outgoing and talkative, he was never afraid to express himself. These characteristics stood him in good stead in 1968, his sophomore year, when he took over the starting quarterback post on the varsity for the injured Terry Hanratty.

In his first start, against Pittsburgh, Joe played a starring role when he completed seven of 10 passes, two for touchdowns, and himself scored two touchdowns in a 56–7 rout. He piloted the Irish to a 34–6 victory over Georgia Tech.

On the second offensive play of a game

against Southern California, he was intercepted for a touchdown. Joe returned to the sidelines and surprised coach Ara Parseghian by saying, "Don't worry, we'll get it back."

"Here I thought we were in a position to get blown out of the Coliseum," Parseghian said later, "and it didn't bother Joe a bit. Before the half was over, Joe had us in front, 21–7. He showed me he had the facility for not being bothered by his mistakes." The final score was 21–21.

It was shortly after Joe's sophomore season that Roger Valdiserri, Notre Dame's sports information director, called Joe into his office.

"How do you pronounce your name?" Roger asked.

"You know, it's THEEZmann," a surprised Joe said.

"Well, from now on it's going to be THIGHS-mann, as in Heisman," declared Valdiserri.

What the sports information director had in mind was the Heisman Trophy, awarded each year to the nation's outstanding college player. Indeed, the young quarterback was already being thought of as a candidate for the trophy.

In his next two seasons Theismann, by now a six-footer weighing 177 pounds, set all sorts of Notre Dame passing records and was named to UPI's All-American team.

His best performance came in a game against Southern California, played in a downpour at the Los Angeles Coliseum. He completed 33 of 58 passes for 526 yards, but Notre Dame lost, 38–28. "The water was cascading down. It just didn't let up. But Joe didn't either. It was the darnedest thing I've ever seen," said coach Parseghian.

During his varsity career Theismann led Notre Dame to 20 victories, only three losses, and two ties. But he didn't win the Heisman; he took second to Stanford quarterback Jim Plunkett in the 1970 voting.

It was a disappointment for Joe, but nobody regarded him as a loser. He was making good grades—3.2 in his senior year—and he was named to the all-academic team based on scholarship and football performance. And, as if in a Hollywood movie script, he married Cheryl Brown, who worked for Roger Valdiserri in the Notre Dame sports publicity office.

His major in college was sociology, but pro football was his goal. The next stop was the National Football League (NFL). Or so Joe thought. There were those who felt he wasn't big enough to make it as a pro quarterback. He didn't get selected in the NFL draft until the fourth round—by the Miami Dolphins.

Unfortunately for Joe, the Dolphins already had young Bob Griese as their quarterback. "My chances of beating him out are one in ten and I won't be happy as a backup quarterback," Theismann said. "And I'm unhappy with some of the provisions of the contract Miami offered me."

So he surprised the football world by signing instead with the Toronto Argonauts of the Canadian Football League. He had three successful years there, but Joe knew he would never be fulfilled until he proved himself in the NFL.

And in 1974 the 24-year-old Theismann returned to the United States as a Washington Redskin in the NFL under coach George Allen. "There is so much to learn," said Theismann, "and I've decided to invest a couple of years getting into the NFL's system."

He couldn't have known, however, that it would take more than two years. The Redskins had veterans Sonny Jurgensen (age 36) and Billy Kilmer (34) at quarterback, and Theismann got to throw only 33 passes in the 1974 and 1975 seasons combined. He did see a little action running back punts. But he didn't start at quarterback until the fifth game of the 1976 season. And it was not until 1978 that he finally won the regular job when Jack Pardee arrived as Redskin coach.

In the first six weeks of the season Washington was unbeaten, but it ended up with an 8-8 record, certainly not good enough to make the playoffs. With the help of assistant coach Joe Walton, Theismann kept improving, and in 1979 he guided the Redskins to a 10-6 mark. In 1980 Theismann, continuing to show his mobility as a passer who could run for yardage when he had to, made the best showing of his NFL career. But the Redskins finished up with only six victories in 16 games.

Under new coach Joe Gibbs in 1981, Joe threw 19 touchdown passes and completed 59.1 percent of his aerials. Nonetheless, the team could manage no better than an 8-8 record.

By now Theismann had become a celebrity in the Washington area—on and off the field. He liked to say, "My mouth has always preceded my performance," and the truth was that he was known for his gift of gab. But he backed up his words with achievements that won him increasing respect in and out of the huddle.

He became a co-host of a Washington morning talk show, in which he interviewed authors, sports figures, and politicians, including Senator Edward Kennedy. He did TV commercials, he owned two restaurants, and he appeared in a movie. And he worked for various community causes, ranging from the United Way and the Cystic Fibrosis Foundation to the Special Olympics. As one writer described him in a magazine article, he "was not your average Joe."

He signed a $1.5-million four-year contract with the Redskins, but he still had something to prove on the football field—that he and the Redskins could win the big game. That was his goal in 1982.

The Redskins assembling around their quarterback in preseason were a magical mix of characters including John Riggins, an independent fullback who for more than a year had refused to talk to the press; an offensive line that called itself the Hogs; and a group of receivers known as the Fun Bunch, whose smallest member, 5-foot-7 Alvin Garrett, was nicknamed Smurf.

In a season shortened by the players' strike Theismann paced the Redskins to an 8-1 record, won the National Football Conference passing title, and was named NFL Man of the Year prior to the Super Bowl against Miami.

As a collegian and professional, Joe had never played on a championship team. "Without the

Theismann smiles with good reason as he holds the Super Bowl trophy won by the Redskins.

title, my career is incomplete," he said on the eve of Super Bowl XVII.

When the final gun sounded in Pasadena, and Washington had won its Super Bowl trophy, Theismann had fulfilled his greatest ambition. In the locker room at first he couldn't stop talking. But after a while, for the first time in his life, he said with a grin: "I'm speechless."

2

KEN ANDERSON
The Bengal from Nowhere

The city of Cincinnati has rarely been as cold as it was on the afternoon of January 10, 1982. The temperature was 9 degrees below zero, and the winds gusting up to 35 miles per hour made it feel like it was 59 degrees below zero. It was certainly no weather to venture outdoors, but the Cincinnati Bengals and the San Diego Chargers had no choice: they were scheduled to meet in the American Football Conference championship game at Riverfront Stadium.

The Cincinnati quarterback, Ken Anderson, knew just how cold it could get in his home park. Anderson had gotten some chilly receptions from Bengal fans in the past, including a brutal booing earlier in the season. But the quarterback had bounced back to have a fine season, guiding his team to its first title game.

Cincinnati's Ken Anderson passed his way into the NFL record book.

But now he would be put to his biggest test: could he throw the ball under these arctic conditions? The Chargers didn't think so; their defense was geared to stop what they thought would be a running rather than a passing game.

The Bengals struck early when Jim Breech booted a 31-yard field goal, and then they got a big break when the Chargers' James Brooks bobbled the next kickoff. Don Bass recovered for the Bengals at the 12-yard line, and two plays later Anderson, ignoring the weather, connected on an eight-yard touchdown pass to M. L. Harris. San Diego came back when Dan Fouts passed to Kellen Winslow for a 33-yard touchdown early in the second quarter, slicing the Cincinnati lead to 10–7.

The cool Bengal quarterback then took his team on a 55-yard drive that resulted in a Pete Johnson touchdown, giving Cincinnati a 17–7 lead at halftime. The second half was more of the same as Anderson helped the Bengals turn the game into a rout. He took the offense on two scoring drives in the half, throwing for a three-yard score to Don Bass to wrap up the 27–7 triumph that put the Bengals in the Super Bowl. Anderson finished with impressive statistics: 14 completions in 22 attempts for 161 yards and two touchdowns.

But it didn't surprise the townfolk in Batavia, Illinois. They'd known for a long time what to expect of Ken Anderson.

He was born in Batavia on February 15, 1949. It's a small town of about 13,000 people located in the northeast portion of the state about 40 miles from Chicago. Ken grew up playing many sports and was encouraged by both his parents. His father, Erik, was the custodian at Batavia High School and would always take time after work to throw a ball around with his son. Anderson's mother, Jean, was a fine athlete in her own right and would often take her son out golfing with her.

It was in the seventh grade that Ken started playing quarterback. At the first practice the coach asked for volunteers to play the position. Anderson was the only youngster to raise his hand, so he became the quarterback. When he moved on to high school, he played three sports—football, basketball, and baseball—and was good enough to earn a starting berth on all three teams.

His buddy on the basketball team was Dan Issel, who went on to become one of the best players in the history of the National Basketball Association. With Issel scoring practically at will, the Batavia basketball team won 28 of 30 games in Ken's junior season. The fact that his father was custodian of the school helped Anderson tremendously—whenever he needed extra practice, his father would go down and open the gym for him.

On the football team Anderson played quarterback and defensive back and was voted an all-conference player at the latter position. Though he had a strong arm, Ken rarely got a chance to show it off, as Batavia relied on a strong running game. "I couldn't understand it," assistant coach Tom Garrey said. "All week long Kenny would throw great in practice and then when the game came, we'd run the ball."

So, as Ken's graduation approached, he was not swamped with scholarship offers. Big-time schools like Notre Dame or the University of Southern California (USC) had no interest in a small-town quarterback with unimpressive statistics.

The only school that showed serious interest in Ken was Augustana College, a school of about 2,000 students in Rock Island, Illinois. But Augustana wasn't interested in Anderson for his football ability; the school offered him a partial scholarship for basketball. Anderson wrote a letter to football coach Ralph Starenko asking if he could try out for the football team.

The coach wrote back that he would be pleased if Ken tried out because "we need good defensive halfbacks." Ken took this as a challenge. He knew he would have to prove that he could play quarterback. He decided to go to Augustana.

In the first game of Anderson's freshman year, he found himself relegated to bench duty as the number 2 quarterback. In the second game of the season, though, the regular quarterback was injured and Anderson got his chance. He threw two touchdowns that day against Augustana–Sioux Falls and started every game after that.

When the football season ended, Anderson played on Augustana's basketball team and was one of the squad's high scorers each year. He found time for his studies, too, maintaining a 3.3 grade-point average while majoring in mathematics.

It was during his sophomore season that pro football scouts began to notice Anderson. That year Kenny completed 136 of 239 passes for 2,117 yards and 20 touchdowns. He also ran for eight more scores. But he failed to receive national recognition due to Augustana's small-college schedule.

One of the pro scouts who came to see Ken

was Bill Walsh, who was working for the Bengals. "I can recall scouting Ken and going to Augustana's homecoming game," said Walsh, who went on to coach the San Francisco 49ers to the National Football League championship. "I pulled my car up to the ticket window and walked right in. There were probably five or six hundred people there. It wasn't hard to spot Ken because he was without doubt the most important player in the stadium."

Though Ken's senior season was cut short due to an injury, Walsh convinced the Bengals that they should take a chance on Anderson in the NFL's 1971 college draft. That's why the Bengals bypassed a quarterback by the name of Joe Theismann to draft Anderson in the third round.

In 1970 the Bengals, in only their third year of existence, had won the American Football Conference (AFC) Central Division title. Their quarterback was Virgil Carter, who had become a favorite due to his daring play. In the eyes of many fans, Carter could do no wrong, but Anderson—who was (and still is) quiet, modest, and shy—was regarded as a newcomer who had to prove himself.

Anderson would have been content to learn by watching in his rookie year (1971), but it didn't turn out that way. The Bengals, after opening the season with a 37–14 bombardment of the Philadelphia Eagles, lost seven games in a row. Carter struggled through a miserable year, and Anderson, who got a chance to play, took the brunt of the blame for the team's shortcomings. "I had to learn to let the boos go in one ear and out the other," he said.

The Bengals finished with a 4-10 record but Anderson had decent statistics for a rookie: 55 percent completions (72 of 131) for 777 yards and five touchdowns. The fans were so rough, however, that Anderson began to think seriously about life after football. He made plans to go back to college in the off-season to pursue a law degree.

In 1972 the Bengals became winners again but Anderson was still booed. Though he completed 57 percent of his passes for almost 2,000 yards, many fans would not forgive Anderson for the team's failure to make the playoffs. Two losses to cross-state rival Cleveland dropped the Bengals to 8-6 and kept them out of post-season play.

It wasn't until 1973 that Anderson began to change the jeers to cheers. He threw for nearly 2,500 yards as Cincinnati went 10-4 and won a playoff berth. The Bengals' stay in the playoffs was a short one, as the Miami Dolphins, en route to a second straight Super Bowl triumph, walloped them, 34–16.

Midway through the 1974 season Anderson wrote his name in the NFL record book. In a game against the Steelers at Riverfront Stadium, Ken completed 16 passes in a row for a record. In the same game he also set another mark by completing 20 of 22 passes for a 90.91 percentage. Though the Bengals suffered through a mediocre 7-7 season, Anderson was brilliant and finished as the AFC's leading passer.

He was a repeat winner in 1975 when the Bengals had their finest season (11-3). In a Monday night game against Buffalo, Anderson completed 30 of 46 passes for a team-record 447 yards as the Bengals defeated the Bills, 33–24. Even stonefaced Paul Brown, the Bengals' coach, was impressed. "Ken Anderson was superb," Brown said, "but that's not unusual."

Anderson, as is his custom, gave all the credit elsewhere. "It was all our receivers," he said. "They did a great job getting open, and if I was throwing the ball right, I should have had 40 completions."

After another fine season in 1976 the bottom fell out for Anderson and the Bengals. In 1977

Ken threw as many interceptions as he did touchdowns (11) and the team had a so-so 8-6 record.

The following season was a nightmare for everyone connected with the Bengals, especially Anderson. He was intercepted a career-high 22 times and the Bengals dropped to 4-12, their worst record since 1968, the team's first season. Fans took their frustrations out on Anderson by booing him. And the Bengals' management was so unhappy with his play that when the 1979 college draft was held, it drafted a quarterback, Jack Thompson of Washington State, in the first round.

Thompson became the new hope in Cincinnati, and Anderson was booed incessantly over the next two years. Things got so bad that Bengal fans cheered when Ken was forced out of a game with an injury in 1980.

While Ken was having his ups and downs on the football field, he was using every spare moment to switch from his playbooks to his law books. And in the summer of 1981 he earned his law degree from Northern Kentucky University's Chase College of Law.

But he wasn't quite ready to give up his favorite sport for the courtroom. As the 1981 season was about to open, Anderson and Thompson were neck and neck for the starting quarter-back position. Only an injury to Thompson settled matters: Anderson would start the opener against the Seattle Seahawks.

The Bengals were favored to beat the Seahawks, but Anderson's first pass was interrupted cepted and returned for a touchdown. By the end of the first quarter Anderson had thrown another interception and the Seahawks had gone in to score. It was 21–0, Seattle, and the Cincinnati fans were down on Anderson. Coach Forrest Gregg yanked him from the game and replaced him with third-stringer Turk Schonert. When the youngster rallied the Bengals to a 27–21 victory, it appeared that Anderson's days as starting quarterback had come to an end.

But three days before the Bengals' next game, Gregg announced that Anderson would start again. That decision, whether it was based on sentiment or luck, was the most important one the coach would make all year. Given a reprieve, Anderson made sure no one would challenge him for the job again.

Leading the attack from his pivotal post as quarterback, Anderson was responsible for the Bengals' becoming the surprise team of the AFC. They won 12 of 16 games and the Central Division title and went on to take the conference championship on that subzero day against San Diego. In his finest season ever, Ken was named 1981 NFL Player of the Year after throwing for 3,754 yards and 29 touchdowns, both career highs for him.

Anderson and his fellow Bengals carried high hopes into the Super Bowl against the San Francisco 49ers on January 24, 1982, at the Silverdome in Pontiac, Michigan.

But it was not to be the day of the Bengal. Ken completed 25 passes for a Super Bowl record, and his team rolled up 356 yards against San Francisco's 275, but in the end the 49ers won out by a 26–21 score.

By now Bill Walsh, the man who had recommended that the Bengals sign Anderson a decade earlier, was coach of San Francisco. And he said, "I have felt all along that Ken is the greatest forward passer in the NFL in recent years."

An even more important tribute came in the winter of 1982 when Ken's hometown of Batavia honored him with a Ken Anderson Day. Students from the high school he had attended made a huge banner that read "We salute Ken Anderson, the Pride of Batavia."

3

ROGER STAUBACH
Straight-Shootin' Cowboy

For Roger Staubach it was like stepping into another world. He had just ended a glittering All-American football career at the U.S. Naval Academy. But unlike most college stars, Staubach didn't move directly into the professional game. When a student graduates from the Naval Academy, he has an obligation to serve four years in the Navy or Marines.

In August 1966 Ensign Staubach got off a helicopter in a strange land of rice paddies and rain forests—Vietnam.

Roger served in the coastal city of Da Nang for a year; his assignments included shipping and receiving freight. It was a full-time job, but Roger didn't forget football completely. After dinner he and Steve Roesinger, a classmate at the Naval Academy, threw passes on a nearby

Dallas' Roger Staubach looks for a receiver as he scampers away from Miami's Bill Stanfill in Super Bowl VI.

Vietnamese soccer field.

After four months in Da Nang, Roger was promoted to lieutenant, junior grade; he was put in charge of 120 men at Chu Lai, a naval supply terminal 60 miles south of Da Nang. It was a big responsibility, with little time off. But after he fulfilled his daily assignments, Roger knew what he had to do. "I ran sprints and threw passes to anybody who'd catch them," he said. "I knew if I could stay in shape in Vietnam, I could certainly do so during my next two years on active duty in the States."

No rookie quarterback had ever returned from four years of service to launch a successful career in professional football. Roger Staubach was the first.

Roger was born on February 5, 1942, and grew up in Silverton, Ohio, a Cincinnati suburb, and a town where kids began to play sports almost as soon as they could walk. In a friendly neighborhood of big backyards and driveway basketball courts, Roger was always involved in as many games as he could.

He developed an immediate lust for competition and a desire to excel. As a nine-year-old Little League baseball player, Roger tried to steal home every time he reached third base. He also asked his coaches if he could play every position.

Although he was smaller than most boys his age, Roger later starred as a catcher and became a key player on a sixth-grade baseball team that won 39 straight games and the state championship.

Roger loved baseball, but during the fall football caught his fancy. With envy he watched the local Catholic Youth Organization team practice in its colorful uniforms, shoulder pads, and shiny helmets. He would imagine himself among them as a star runner, squirming through tacklers and scoring last-minute touchdowns. But because of his size, his parents— Bob, a shoe-store sales manager, and Betty Staubach—wouldn't allow Roger to play football until he reached 125 pounds in the seventh grade.

Besides, the Staubachs wanted their only child to try activities other than sports so he could then choose a career from a variety of things. When he was 10, he took piano lessons. His teacher, Helen Randolph, kept telling his mother what a great pianist he was going to be. Yet Roger couldn't wait for his lessons to end, because there was always a neighborhood game going on.

When Roger was 12, he got pinched up in a tuxedo for his first—and last—piano recital in a big Cincinnati music hall. When Roger forgot the notes to the William Tell Overture, a piece he had practiced and memorized for hours, his parents decided he should probably go back to his first love—sports.

Between the eighth grade and his freshman year at Purcell High School, Roger suddenly shot up to six feet, and gained 40 pounds to reach about 160. It seemed natural that Roger attend Purcell, a private Catholic school for boys. He was very serious about his religion, even at age 13, and it just so happened Purcell also fielded outstanding football teams.

When over 100 kids went out for the freshman team—with most trying out for halfback— Roger chose to be an end. "I knew there were two things I could do—catch the ball and run with it," he said. "Since everybody wanted to carry the ball, the halfback line was the longest. I picked end, because it was the shortest line."

The next year head coach Jim McCarthy had other ideas. Only seniors, he said, deserved the glory of playing offense for the varsity.

Roger wasn't exactly thrilled by being switched to defensive halfback, but he didn't sulk. Besides, he still had baseball and basket-ball, and in those sports there was little grade-level distinction.

In Roger's senior year, however, his full foot-ball talents were finally realized. Coach McCarthy made him the number 1 quarter-back, but not because of his arm. "We didn't have many passing plays called, but I think I gained over five hundred yards running the ball," said Roger. "I'd just start taking off after I'd drop back to pass. It just came naturally to me."

Roger's wild zigzagging runs past fallen tacklers earned him the nickname Roger the Dodger. His best high-school game was when Purcell played crosstown rival Elder High for the city championship. It was a game Roger dedicated to his dad, who was hospitalized for diabetes.

Purcell fans will never forget Roger's per-formance. On one play Roger surprised every-one, including his coach, when he faked a hand-off and ran 62 yards for the touchdown that won the game, 20–14.

He was a star now, but always modest. His classmates elected him student body president and prom king. In the eyes of his teammates he was a leader. And by the end of his senior year more than 30 colleges had offered him scholar-ships.

Ohio State and Purdue were among the tradi-tional powerhouses heavily recruiting Roger. But he was really hoping to go to Notre Dame, a Catholic university of legendary football fame. It was also the college he had rooted for since his boyhood. But Notre Dame coach Joe Kuharich told Roger, "Sorry, our quarterback scholar-ships have been used up."

When Roger and his parents returned from a weekend trip to the U.S. Naval Academy in An-napolis, Maryland, his mind was made up. "The whole atmosphere at the Naval Academy was better than what I had seen at other schools," he said. "When I went out to a game with some midshipmen, they mostly talked about the im-portance of studies and education. I was im-pressed."

When Roger got back home, a Notre Dame scout called. "A quarterback scholarship has opened," he said.

"I'm sorry, sir," Roger replied. "But I'm going to go to Navy."

But not right away. Though he always made excellent grades in science and math, Roger had not developed good study habits in high school. He soon learned he couldn't get into the

Naval Academy because he had scored poorly on the English part of his entrance exam. Now he had to make another decision. Should he go to a different school? Or should he go to a junior college for a year, study hard, and take the exam again?

Roger chose the hard route. He attended New Mexico Military Institute (NMMI) for a year. On the football field Roger ran and passed NMMI to a 9-1 record and made Junior College All-American. But in the classroom he worked even harder. After a year in the desert country he was ready to become a midshipman.

Roger immediately joined the plebe (freshman) football team, whose main job was to play the varsity team in practice during the week to prepare it for the weekend game. The very first time he got the ball in a scrimmage against the varsity, Roger scored a touchdown on one of his darting scrambles. He continued to run where he wanted all afternoon. After ordering extra tackling practice the next day, coach Wayne Hardin realized it wasn't the defense's fault. "It's that kid Staubach," he told an assistant. "He's amazing."

Roger wasn't eligible to play for the varsity in 1961, his plebe year. And the next season he watched the first few games from the bench—

anxiously waiting for his chance. Then in a game against Cornell in which neither team moved the ball, Hardin signaled to Roger. "Get in there and move us, Roger," he called.

The Annapolis crowd of 23,000 roared when it saw the sophomore wearing the number 12 navy-blue jersey trot into the huddle. The fans had heard about the promising newcomer.

And Roger didn't disappoint. In 23 minutes he ran for two touchdowns and passed for another. Roger personally accounted for 188 yards as Navy swamped Cornell, 41–0.

Roger's performance fired up the school. The Big Game—Army vs. Navy—was coming up. More than any other college football rivalry, this game belonged to the students.

Army had a very solid team and was favored, but feeling ran sky-high on the Navy campus. The midshipmen had frenzied pep rallies for two weeks and couldn't stop talking about their cool quarterback. They even hung a huge banner on Bancroft Hall that read "Home of Roger Staubach."

Over 98,000 fans—including a former PT boat skipper named John F. Kennedy—turned out for the 1962 Army-Navy classic. And on that brisk December day, Roger again didn't disappoint. To the joy of President Kennedy and the other Navy rooters, Roger and his teammates destroyed Army, 34–14.

It was all a fitting prelude to the next season, when Roger won the Heisman Trophy, which is awarded to the best college football player in the nation.

As a senior in 1964 Roger suffered a leg injury in the very first game, a 21–8 victory over Penn State, and hobbled his way through much of the season. But he came back to lead Navy to a 27–14 victory over Duke that broke a winless string of six games.

Before graduation the Dallas Cowboys of the NFL got in touch with Roger. They knew he couldn't play for them for four more years because of his military commitment. But they took a gamble. The Cowboys agreed to pay Roger $5,000 a year during his four-year hitch in the Navy. They hoped that he would eventually choose to play pro ball rather than make the Navy his career.

During Roger's first year in the Navy he married his longtime sweetheart, Marianne, whom he had met when she was an eighth-grade cheerleader.

After his service in Vietnam the Navy gave him a two-week leave so he could spend time at Dallas' rookie camp in Thousand Oaks, California. He was still in the Navy, but he was able to work out briefly with the Cowboys. More important, his performance at the camp would determine if he still had the skills and quickness to pursue a pro career. Roger's passing and running impressed the Cowboy coaches. And he satisfied his own mind—he felt he could make the grade.

In 1969 Roger was discharged from the Navy. At the same time Don Meredith—Dallas' main quarterback for most of its nine-year history—retired. Roger reported to camp and became the number 2 quarterback, backing up starter Craig Morton.

In his first two seasons with the Cowboys, Roger played very little. So before Dallas played Baltimore in Super Bowl V in January 1971; Roger pondered his future. He was almost 29 years old, and he still hadn't had a chance to prove his talents.

One week before the game a reporter asked Roger how he felt. "I'm the backup quarterback on a Super Bowl team," he replied. "But that doesn't mean I like it."

Dallas wound up losing by 16–13 to Baltimore in the Super Bowl, and there were many critics who said that the Cowboys buckled under pressure in the "big" games.

Coach Tom Landry had hesitated at giving Roger more playing time. "It usually takes a quarterback three to five years to develop," he said.

But he felt that Roger was equal to Craig Morton and he decided to rotate them in the 1971 season. Clearly, every move Staubach made was being closely watched. In one exhibition game against Philadelphia he was spun around by a huge defensive lineman named Mel Tom—and then clobbered by Tom's forearm. It was a cheap shot, Roger thought, and he said so when the incident was replayed on the game films.

"I'd like to get that guy in a back alley sometime," said Roger.

"But he's over six-four and weighs over two-fifty," someone said. "What would you do with him in a back alley?"

"Look," said Roger. "I've got four years of hand-to-hand combat I never got to use."

Roger surprised people with this burst of anger. Ordinarily a soft-spoken gentleman, he was obviously feeling the pressure. Meanwhile, his Cowboy teammates were feeling a similar pressure from the fans and media to become a championship team.

When Landry finally decided midway

through the season that Roger would be number 1, the Cowboys rode to new heights. Roger led them to seven straight regular-season wins, two more in the playoffs, and a berth in Super Bowl VI.

Their opponents were the Miami Dolphins. The place was Tulane Stadium, in New Orleans. The stigma of not winning "the big one" had haunted the Dallas Cowboys like a bad dream. Miami, on the other hand, was a young and talented team in just its sixth season of existence.

On Super Sunday the atmosphere was charged with anticipation. As some of the 80,000-plus fans were filing in, a man at the ticket gate was talking to Commodore Paul Borden, a classmate of Roger's at the Naval Academy.

"Boy, this is Staubach's first Super Bowl," said the man. "If any Cowboy is going to feel the pressure, it's him."

The commodore shook his head. "This is a big game," he said. "But I'm not sure how much bigger it is in comparison to the Army-Navy games Roger played in. Every midshipman, every officer—why, every admiral in the fleet—they were all on Roger's shoulders. But he thrives on pressure. He seems to respond to it perfectly."

Perfectly, indeed. Roger was magnificent in Super Bowl VI; his passing was like clockwork and his dashing runs befuddled Miami's defense. The final score was Dallas 24, Miami 3, and Roger was named the game's Most Valuable Player (MVP).

When Roger emerged from the dressing room, he was met by hundreds of well-wishers who serenaded the former Navy officer with a chorus of "Anchors Aweigh," the Navy fight song.

Throughout the 1970s Roger continued to capture the imagination of pro football fans with his supreme passing and running and his uncanny flair for dramatic finishes.

One of those occurred on the frozen turf at Minnesota during the 1975 playoffs. Dallas was trailing, 14–10, in the last seconds. On the final play of the game Roger escaped the grasp of two Viking tacklers and uncorked a 60-yard bomb that receiver Drew Pearson somehow managed to catch on his hip for a touchdown. Roger called that his "Hail Mary" pass because his prayer was answered. And because of it the Cowboys earned another trip to the Super Bowl, in January 1976 in Los Angeles.

In Super Bowl X against the defending champion Pittsburgh Steelers, Roger almost engineered another miracle of sorts. He threw a touchdown pass to Percy Howard late in the game and was driving the Cowboys toward another score. But on the next-to-last play of the game, another pass to Howard went off his fingertips and Dallas lost a heartbreaker, 21–17.

But in January 1978, in New Orleans, Staubach and his Cowboys defeated Denver, 27–10, in Super Bowl XII. Staubach's pass to Butch Johnson, who made a great end-zone catch, broke open the game in the third quarter.

The following season was a rough one for Roger, who at age 36 suffered a series of concussions. But he nearly pulled off another upset in Super Bowl XIII against Pittsburgh in Miami. Roger threw three touchdown passes, two of them within a little more than two minutes of each other in the fourth period, but the Steelers finally won out, 35–31.

Under Staubach's leadership Dallas had become recognized as America's most popular team. His teammates knew why.

"We were always the clean-cut team," said Cliff Harris, the Cowboys' all-pro safety. "It's all because of Roger. We developed *his* image. That's what Roger is, Captain America."

In the spring of 1980, 38-year-old Roger Staubach called a press conference in Dallas. His short wavy hair neatly trimmed as it was way back in his Navy days, the scrambling master of the Cowboys announced that it was at last time to retire.

But nobody could ever call Roger the Dodger a quitter.

4

DAN FOUTS
The Ball Boy Who
Became a Charger

It was a day that the San Diego Chargers and their star quarterback, Dan Fouts, had looked forward to for a long time. It was January 11, 1981, and they were playing the Oakland Raiders for the AFC championship. The winner would play in Super Bowl XV.

San Diego had won the 1963 title in the old American Football League but the team had never been this close to a championship berth in the NFL. And now it was the favorite, playing at home against a team that had finished second behind San Diego in the AFC's Western Division.

But everything seemed to go wrong for the Chargers. Led by quarterback Jim Plunkett, the

Starting as a ball boy, Dan Fouts learned from the masters and grew up to be pass-master of the San Diego Chargers.

Raiders jumped off to an early lead, and no matter what Fouts and his teammates did, Oakland turned things to its advantage. Although Fouts passed for 336 yards, two of his passes were intercepted and his team's running game was futile. There was no stopping the Raiders, who downed the Chargers, 34–27, in a game more one-sided than the score indicates.

It was the worst of times for Dan Fouts. Limp with fatigue, frustrated by defeat, he sat in front of his locker. Disappointment was nowhere more visible than on Dan's bearded face.

Reporters pressed in, wanting to know from Fouts why the Chargers had lost the game. Fouts wanted to know himself. He answered each question as best he could, giving praise to the Raiders. Now the only thing Dan Fouts wanted to do was disappear into his home in the wilds of Indian Ford, Oregon.

A microphone was suddenly thrust in front of Fouts, about a half-inch from his nose. His expression instantly changed from disappointment to irritability.

"Get that microphone out of my face," he snapped.

Then Dan Fouts broke into a smile. "Hi, Dad."

Bob Fouts works out of San Francisco, where

Dan was reared, and one of his jobs is to cover major sporting events on the West Coast for ABC radio. This often brings him mike-to-face with his own son, the record-breaking quarterback.

Dan Fouts holds the NFL single-season records for pass attempts, completions, and passing yardage. He set these marks in 1981, beating his own records. During the 1981 season Fouts established 13 NFL or Charger records. It seemed he was born to play quarterback.

Not so. In the beginning Fouts wanted to play end. He was tall, skinny, and, he says, "I could catch the ball a whole lot better than I could throw it." But his father insisted he play quarterback.

Dan Fouts bowed to experience. His father knew a budding quarterback when he saw one. Bob Fouts was around quarterbacks all the time as play-by-play announcer for the San Francisco 49ers.

From the time he was barely in grammar school until he graduated from St. Ignatius High School in San Francisco, Dan also was around the 49ers. He was born on June 10, 1951, in San Francisco. He lived a boyhood dream every day, mingling with the great

49ers—Joe Perry, Hugh McElhenny, Y.A. Tittle, Leo Nomellini, John Brodie—at their summer training camp on the St. Mary's College campus in Moranga, California.

Dan's job was ball boy. He didn't see how you could call it a job. Being around his idols—how could this be work? It was pure fun seven days a week.

Each year Bob Fouts would take one of his five children east for the 49ers' game in Baltimore, swinging by Washington, D.C., to see the nation's capital. Dan's turn came in 1962, when he was in the sixth grade, and it turned out that he got a bonus. The San Francisco Giants were in the World Series, and young Dan—a Little League shortstop—got to see a game at Yankee Stadium in New York.

When he came back home, he wrote about the whole experience for a class report.

It was about this time that Dan thought he might like to play football. He threw the ball with accuracy at St. Brendan's School, so he decided to try Pop Warner football—the football equivalent of Little League baseball.

The coach showed up the first day to look over the new team of Drake Junior Pirates. He made them run 20 laps, and that was it for the initial practice. The Drake Junior Pirates turned out for the second day of workouts, but no coach. He had quit without telling anyone. The father of one of the Pirates had to take over the coaching.

At St. Ignatius High, Dan ran the 120-yard high hurdles in 15.2 and played forward on the school's championship basketball team. He was also doing his ball-boy chores during the football season for the 49ers.

One Sunday at a 49er game St. Ignatius football coach Vince Tringali saw a lanky youngster throw a perfect spiral to an official. When he inquired about the player, Tringali learned that he attended St. Ignatius. Tringali invited Fouts out for football—and that's how Dan's career really began.

Once he got into the sport, Dan was all seriousness. He began lifting weights to build up his 6-foot-1, 145-pound frame. He never drank or smoked, not even a glass of champagne at his high-school graduation.

"He was a fierce competitor," his father said. "When he played with his brothers or relatives, he played to win. I wouldn't want to play basketball against him because he'd knock me on my behind."

"My father was competitive too," Dan said. "I wouldn't want to play basketball against him either because he might do something that would make me want to knock him on his behind."

Bob Fouts believes that his son's toughness may have developed from walking to high school through tough neighborhoods. Dan feels that it wasn't so much the neighborhoods, but the strict Jesuit teachers at St. Ignatius, who steeled his nerves and defined his direction.

Of course, when you're the fourth of five children, Dan noted, "you have situations where you have to get something and . . ."

You become competitive.

From the streets of San Francisco, Dan Fouts took his strong passing arm to the great outdoors. The University of Oregon at Eugene was the only school to offer Fouts a scholarship.

Oregon must have seen something in Fouts that every other school missed. Fouts turned out for the varsity like any young, eager candidate, but something separated him from the other quarterbacks. It was the same characteristic that would separate him from other quarterbacks in the NFL record book: toughness. He set 49 school offense records, including career passing yardage (5,995 yards) and touchdown passes (37). Fouts was named All-Pacific-8 Conference, All-Coast, and was selected to play in the East-West Shrine Game and the Senior Bowl.

The next step for Daniel Francis Fouts would be the NFL, though there wasn't a mad rush to acquire his services in 1973. The San Diego Chargers waited until the third round to draft him. He was the sixty-fourth player taken, and the sixth quarterback—behind Bert Jones, Gary Huff, Ron Jaworski, Gary Keithly, and Joe Ferguson.

The reason Fouts was taken so low had nothing to do with his passing arm. He looked frail, and there was doubt whether he could take the physical pounding of the NFL. When he dropped back to pass in the pocket, he looked like a man who was stumbling and about to fall. What the NFL scouts couldn't see in Fouts's rating chart was his toughness and competitiveness.

More than that, he was a leader, with great personal confidence. Soon he would remind others of the great 49er quarterback John Brodie, because their personalities were so similar. Fouts took this comparison as a compliment, since he had looked up to Brodie during his ball-boy years. Now that Fouts was an NFL rookie, he called on Brodie for advice.

"They'll tell you that you need three to five

years to develop," Brodie told him. "But the best way to develop is to play."

During Fouts's rookie year in 1973, the Chargers were made up chiefly of veteran players of marginal ability and/or little time left in the NFL. San Diego's oldest player was the incomparable Johnny Unitas, playing his final season with the Chargers after many glorious years in Baltimore.

Unitas taught Fouts how to read defenses and instructed him on the general ins and outs of the game. Fouts learned something every day just by watching the elder statesman at work.

But as John Brodie had said, you learn more by playing than watching. In the fourth game of the season, at Pittsburgh, Unitas and backup quarterback Wayne Clark couldn't get the Chargers moving against the famous Steel Curtain defense. At halftime Pittsburgh led, 38–0. Fouts made his professional debut, completing 11 of 21 passes for 174 yards and one touchdown. He directed two other scoring drives as the Chargers lost.

"You may have seen the emergence of a star quarterback," San Diego owner Gene Klein said after the game. "The kid was somethin' out there, wasn't he? I mean, he was really somethin'."

Pittsburgh was similarly impressed. Coach Chuck Noll raved about Fouts's play, and other Steelers said that it was time for a change in San Diego—from Unitas to Fouts.

Fouts started the next game, against Oakland. Over his first three years in the NFL, Fouts threw 16 touchdown passes. He also threw 36 interceptions. He was learning, all right, but he needed more instruction.

In 1976 Bill Walsh came from Cincinnati to San Diego as offensive coordinator. Dan Fouts became his foremost project. "He rebuilt me from the ground floor up," Fouts would later say. "Everything I am in pro football, I owe to Bill Walsh."

Walsh taught Fouts how to use the field and his receivers, then gave him more receivers by sending four and five men into pass patterns. Walsh spent only one year in San Diego, but he left with an indelible impression of Fouts.

"Dan has tremendous toughness," said Walsh, repeating the all too familiar word. "It's tough fiber. Dan is the strongest force in the NFL from the standpoint of dynamic leadership and productivity."

Words spoken by a man who has remade many a quarterback into a yardage producer, a winner. Walsh later took another third-round draft pick, Joe Montana, and reshaped him into a Super Bowl quarterback, the leader of the 49ers' championship team in 1981.

The 6-foot-3 Fouts built himself up to 205 pounds during the Walsh period. Gone was the frailty that detractors always mentioned. Greatness was around the corner. Fouts passed for 2,535 yards in 1976, but the Chargers had a 6-8 won-lost record. The frustration of playing with a losing team led to his voluntary retirement the next season. His intention was for the Chargers to trade him, but they refused to let a quarterback of his growing stature get away. Fouts rejoined the team for the eleventh game of the 1977 season.

Offensive-minded Don Coryell replaced Tommy Prothro as the Chargers' coach during the 1978 season, and Fouts's career took off. His touchdown passes per season from 1978 to 1982 read 24, 24, 30, 33, and 17. His passing yardage increased from 2,999 to 4,082 to 4,715 and 4,802, then dropped to 2,889 in 1982.

No matter how rough things ever look for the Chargers, no matter what the score is or how many times Fouts has been intercepted, he has the remarkable ability to pick himself and the team up and come firing back. Fouts—and this is the mark of a true quarterback—is even better when he is behind than when he is ahead.

For this reason he is the most feared quarterback in the game as well as one of the most respected. His competitiveness never allows him to quit. The only way to stop Dan Fouts is to not let him have the football.

And to think that at one time he wanted to play end. It's a good thing that father knew best.

5

JOE NAMATH
Jet Bomber

Try as he might to concentrate on his studies, there were those moments when the young boy's mind would wander away to a world of excitement. Sitting in a classroom in the small town of Beaver Falls, Pennsylvania, this slight youth with the tousled hair and faraway look would daydream about being a professional football player.

One day a teacher interrupted his reverie. Always honest with himself and others, the youngster told the teacher about his most secret desire. The teacher, staring down at the boy, responded with a stern lecture about wasting precious time on impossible goals.

"But I never stopped dreaming," the boy later admitted. And as he grew older and

The New York Jets' Joe Namath pitches out against Baltimore in Super Bowl III.

stronger, he did more than just dream. He worked hard, developing a muscular body and the skills that would give him the chance to fulfill his ambition.

"If you want something bad enough," Joe Namath says now, "you'll get it if you work for it."

Even for Joe Namath, surely one of the great quarterbacks of all time and certainly one of the most flamboyant, his incredible talent did not come as a gift.

Joe was born May 31, 1943, in Beaver Falls, a steel town 30 miles northwest of Pittsburgh. He was the youngest of four sons in a Hungarian-American household, and his father worked in a steel mill. The Namaths were an athletic family, and Joe excelled in baseball and basketball.

As for football, he was barely good enough to make his high-school team as a sophomore. Joe was the smallest member of the Beaver Falls High School team. In the entire season he got to play two minutes, and that was on defense. The following year he was elevated to starting quarterback, but was so ineffective that he lost the job after three games.

The next summer, having determined that it took a lot of hard work to make dreams come true, Joe pushed himself every day to develop his skills to the fullest.

That fall, in his senior year, Joe won the quarterback job, and this time he kept it. He completed 85 of 146 passes for 1,564 yards and, most important, he led his team to the Western Pennsylvania championship.

Joe made all-state and discovered for the first time what it was like to be a celebrity. Soon he would have to decide between football and baseball.

A strong-hitting outfielder, he had been offered baseball contracts by the St. Louis Cardinals, Baltimore Orioles, Kansas City A's, and Chicago Cubs. The Cubs offered him $50,000, which seemed a fortune to a poor boy who came from a steel town, but Joe's family insisted he go to college.

Namath received numerous college offers and eventually settled on Alabama, where he came under the influence of Paul (Bear) Bryant, who would become the winningest coach in college football history.

At first Joe was very unhappy so far from home. But with his open, easygoing manner, Joe soon made friends, and he enjoyed playing football under Bryant. In Namath's three varsity seasons Alabama lost only four games, and in his senior year, despite a knee injury that was to affect his entire career, Joe completed 64 percent of his passes. Namath climaxed his college career by leading the Tide past Texas in the 1965 Orange Bowl, a victory that clinched the national championship.

Along with developing the basic skills, Namath absorbed one very simple lesson from Bryant, who drilled it into his young prize: "You play to win and to hate even the thought of losing."

Until he tore ligaments in his right knee in a game against North Carolina State in his senior year, Namath was a strong running threat. But his powerful, accurate arm and intelligent play as a quarterback overrode all else. On top of that, his colorful personality made Joe a favorite of the fans. All of which added up in 1965 to make him the most highly sought prize in the war between the long-established National Football League and the young American Football League (AFL).

Sonny Werblin, himself a showman of note and the owner at that time of the AFL's New York Jets, took a big gamble by offering Namath a $427,000 contract. Joe readily agreed to it, and thus was born the legend of "Broadway Joe."

"I needed to build a franchise with somebody

who could do more than just play," Werblin said.

The size of Joe's contract was unheard of in those days, causing comedian Bob Hope to quip, "Joe Namath's the only quarterback in history who'll play in a business suit."

Less than a month after signing the contract, Namath underwent surgery for the first time to remove cartilage from his right knee. Dr. James Nicholas, the team physician, estimated at the time that Namath would last no more than five years.

Instead, although Namath had to endure more knee operations, he had a 13-season career in which his courage matched his ability.

Weeb Ewbank, Namath's coach on the Jets, was one of those who knew firsthand what Joe endured.

"His knees were very bad," Ewbank said. "Most players wouldn't even have dressed with problems like that. Sometimes he could barely walk, but he dressed and tried to play. I really gained admiration for that man."

When Namath first joined the Jets, his veteran teammates showed natural resentment at the money and attention this wise-guy rookie was receiving. Adding to his problems, Namath's knee prevented him from taking part in the burdensome running exercises during training camp.

Realizing full well that the team's welfare was at stake, Namath felt it was necessary to clear the air during a club meeting. Joe told his teammates, "All I'm asking is that you don't judge me for the money or the publicity, that you let me get out on the field and play football."

This session helped bring the club together and was a sample of how Namath was to charm and win over his teammates.

Given the chance to prove himself on the field, Namath did just that—with a style that was peculiarly his. He had a remarkably quick release of the ball and could successfully throw while off balance or while drifting to the side. In addition, his fingers are extraordinarily long, and this allowed him to fake a pass—causing the defenders to commit themselves—and then hold on to the ball for another instant until he had a clear field.

As a rookie Namath was the third leading passer in the AFL with 164 completions in 340 attempts for 18 touchdowns and 2,220 yards. In the next four years he never fell below a 49 percent completion rate for any season.

Namath's peak came in 1968. In that year he

helped shape the history of professional football.

In 1967 he had established career highs with 4,007 passing yards and 26 TD passes. He continued to shine in 1968 when he carried the Jets to their first AFL championship. Still, the Jets weren't expected to do much against the NFL's Baltimore Colts in Super Bowl III, played on January 12, 1969.

In the week leading up to the game, Namath enraged a lot of people by flatly stating, "We are going to win. I guarantee it."

And win it the Jets did. Before an unbelieving crowd of 75,377 in Miami's Orange Bowl stadium, Namath completed 17 of 28 passes for 206 yards and was voted the Most Valuable Player in a stunning 16–7 victory.

For the first time, the AFL was able to put itself on an equal footing with the NFL.

There was another memorable game against Baltimore in 1972 when Namath threw six touchdown passes, but there were also numerous injuries. A broken bone in his right wrist in 1970 and severe ligament damage to his left knee in a 1971 exhibition limited him to a total of nine games in those two years.

Through it all "Broadway Joe" remained the most visible and exciting player in football. In 1972 he signed a two-year contract for half a million dollars, making him the highest paid quarterback in football, and after playing out his option in 1974, he agreed in 1975 to another two-year pact worth $900,000, establishing him at the time as the best paid player in NFL history.

Namath closed out his career with the Los Angeles Rams in 1977, appearing in just four games for them. At 34, and with so much of his life before him, he wasn't ready to accept a

His fans cheered "Broadway Joe" in New York on the day they honored the Super Bowl champion Jets.

backup role, and he left the game with dignity.

In his 13-year career Namath appeared in 140 games, completing 1,886 of 3,762 pass attempts for 27,663 yards and 173 TD's. His completion percentage was 50.1.

Unquestionably, Joe Namath was the most written about player of his era. He admittedly liked the good life, was a rambling storyteller, and enjoyed being in the public eye. His loyalty to friends and teammates was admirable, and he was known to be remarkably honest. Often he claimed that things written and said about him were exaggerated, but this was part of the image that he inspired. Consider, for example, the title of his autobiography, *I Can't Wait Until Tomorrow 'Cause I Get Better Looking Every Day.*

This same image provided him with another high-paying career, one where bad knees wouldn't hamper him. Namath became one of the most sought-after personalities for television commercial work—the most memorable was a commercial in which he wore pantyhose.

There also followed a new life with Namath appearing in films and television shows. The widespread popularity he had earned in football and his genuine outgoing personality proved to be valuable assets in show business.

"I feel as if I have to keep proving myself every day," said the man who had already achieved so much. "I have to prove myself to myself. I have a conscience and I feel guilty if I don't do a lot of great things every single day."

6

JOE MONTANA
The 49ers' Comeback Kid

Joe Montana could hear the roar of the crowd as he lay shivering on the floor of the Notre Dame locker room. Houston had scored again, widening its lead over the Fighting Irish in the Cotton Bowl game on New Year's Day, 1979.

It was the final game of Montana's college football career, and here he was wrapped in blankets and being fed chicken soup while his teammates were getting chewed up out on the field. He was cut and bleeding from the rock salt used to clear the field after an ice storm struck Dallas, dropping the temperature to 17 degrees. Montana's temperature had also dropped—to 96 degrees—and the alarmed Notre Dame coaches had made him stay in the locker room at the start of the second half.

The home remedy worked, and Montana returned to action late in the third quarter. With eight minutes left, Houston led, 34–12. But this was the type of situation in which Joe Montana thrived. He ran for one touchdown and threw for another, adding a two-point conversion pass. Now, with no time left on the clock, he hit Kris Haines with an eight-yard pass to make it 34–33, Houston. Then he found Haines again for the two-point conversion that capped one of college football's great comebacks.

Such last-second heroics—which had earned him the nickname "The Comeback Kid"—were nothing new for Joe Montana. Carl Crawley, who coached young Joe in midget football back in Monongahela, Pennsylvania, remembers a game the 80-pound quarterback pulled out with a 30-yard pass. "That's long for a kid," Crawley pointed out. "Even then, he had that kind of excitement."

Joe Montana, who was born on June 11, 1956, in New Eagle, Pennsylvania, had always been excited about sports. Theresa Montana remembers that her husband "had Joey throwing footballs when he was four years old. One of the earliest memories I have of him is toddling around the house with a ball in his hand—a baseball in summer, then a football, then a big basketball in the winter. When my husband

San Francisco's Joe Montana prepares to pass against Cincinnati in Super Bowl XVI.

wasn't home, Joey was always pestering some-one to throw him the ball."

When he was eight, Joe made the midget league football team, but he didn't become a starter right away. Ahead of him was Paul Timko, a bigger and stronger quarterback. Once, after a long run, Joe "really got whacked" and broke down in tears. But when he lowered his head and cracked his helmet, coach Crawley knew his little quarterback was ready. Timko went to the bench.

At Ringgold High School, Joe had to prove himself all over again. The starting quarterback was the same Paul Timko he had beaten out years before. At the start of his junior year in 1972, Joe turned in his game jersey and threat-ened to transfer to nearby Butler because his coaches considered him too frail to be num-ber 1.

Montana made his point and won the job. His first start was against arch-rival Monessen, which had smothered Ringgold, 54–6, the year before. With Montana throwing four touch-down passes—three to a converted tight end named Paul Timko—Ringgold fought Mones-sen to a 34–34 tie.

Ringgold went on to a 4-3-2 record that year with Montana behind center—most of the time.

Once he lost concentration and lined up behind a guard. The center snapped the ball straight up in the air. Joe caught it and made two yards on the play, demonstrating his ability to react in a crisis.

Although as a senior Joe led Ringgold to an 8-1 record and a league co-championship, Joe didn't immediately gain what he wanted more than anything—a football scholarship to Notre Dame.

His earliest childhood memory is not of his mother's voice, but the voices of the Notre Dame announcers. Every Saturday in the fall when Joe was growing up, his father had every radio in the house tuned to the Notre Dame game. It follows that when young Joe played catch with a neighborhood pal, he would pretend to be Terry Hanratty throwing to Jim Seymour (the Notre Dame battery in those days).

But when Montana was a senior in high school, Notre Dame recruiters didn't exactly knock down his door. A three-sport star, he was ready to go to North Carolina State on a basketball scholarship (he was an all-state guard) when the Irish finally came calling.

But Montana didn't get the call too often during his first year at Notre Dame. He was one of seven quarterbacks on the junior varsity and threw just six passes, completing one for 35 yards. The first pass he threw in varsity competition was intercepted, and by the end of the season he was tenth string.

Montana had fought his way up to second-string status by the following fall. He replaced starter Rick Slager and led the Irish to a 31–7 victory over Northwestern, but still couldn't gain the number 1 job. Against North Carolina, he entered the game in the fourth quarter with Notre Dame trailing, 14–6. Joe completed three of four passes for 129 yards, including an 80-yarder to Ted Burgmeier with 1:23 left that gave the Irish a 21–14 victory.

The next week he came off the bench again with Notre Dame trailing Air Force Academy, 30–10, going into the fourth quarter. Montana threw for three touchdowns—the last with 3:23 remaining—and Notre Dame won, 31–30.

But Joe chipped a finger in the Navy game and missed the final three games of the season. Then in preseason practice in 1976, he suffered a shoulder separation and had to sit out the year.

When he came back in 1977, he was a third-stringer. Coach Dan Devine thought his junior quarterback had a dead arm, and it sometimes seemed that way.

In the Purdue game Rusty Lisch got off to a

poor start and was replaced by Gary Forystek. When the second-stringer got hurt, Montana figured it was his turn. But Lisch came trotting back onto the field.

Finally, with Notre Dame behind, 24–10, late in the third quarter, Devine sent Montana into the game. When his teammates saw him run onto the field, they let out a resounding cheer, several of them jumping up and down. They knew that if anyone could pull out the game, it was Joe Montana. And he did just that, connecting on 9 of 14 passes for 154 yards—putting three TD's on the board in six minutes—and the Irish won, 31–24.

Dan Devine was finally convinced. "The team responded to him," the coach said, "and I responded to him." Montana became the starter and led Notre Dame to eight straight wins—the last a 38–10 trouncing of Texas in the Cotton Bowl—and the national championship.

The Montana magic was missing early in the 1978 season, and the Irish lost to Michigan and Missouri. But Joe pulled out a game against Pittsburgh by engineering 19 points in a six-minute stretch during the second half for a 26–17 victory. Then, in his final regular-season game against USC, he overcame a 24–6 half-time deficit to give Notre Dame the lead, only to see the Trojans win on a last-second field goal. Then came the Cotton Bowl miracle that certified Montana as a genuine Notre Dame legend in the tradition of Knute Rockne, George Gipp, Frank Leahy, and Rocky Bleier.

Now Montana was ready for the pros, but they weren't all that eager to grab him. After the Cotton Bowl, Montana, who had earned his business administration/marketing degree in December, moved to Southern California. Cathleen (Cass) Castillo, an airlines flight attendant based in Los Angeles, was one of his incentives for moving. But there was also the chance that he might land a job with one of the NFL teams on the West Coast.

Before the college draft Montana had a tryout with the Los Angeles Rams, who dismissed him with a "nice kid, no arm" rating.

But Montana continued to work out on the beach with UCLA receiver James Owens, who was coveted by the San Francisco 49ers. The 49ers' new coach, Bill Walsh, gave Joe a tryout, and two days later drafted him in the third round.

Walsh liked Montana's grace under pressure, his ability to wait until the last moment to throw a pass. "He's like a great writer or musician," the coach said. "A great asset can have a counterpoint to it. Sometimes he would wait too long and throw a bad pass. I suppose the so-called experts call that inconsistency instead of saying, 'Look at that marvelous quality. If we can only channel it.' "

Walsh took his time in developing the young quarterback. Montana threw only 23 passes as a rookie in 1979. He began the next season as the backup to Steve DeBerg, who had a strong arm but a tendency to throw interceptions under pressure.

When the 49ers played the Jets in New York on September 21, 1980, DeBerg had laryngitis. He was equipped with a special amplifier system fitted under his uniform so he could be heard in the huddle.

In the first quarter the 49ers had the ball at the Jets' five-yard line when DeBerg left the game, supposedly to have the amplifier fixed. In came Montana, who had not played at all in the 49ers' first two games. On the first play Montana slipped around the right side for a touchdown.

In the second quarter Montana replaced DeBerg again. This time he passed 20 yards to Dwight Clark for a TD. In the third quarter Montana came in again and hit Clark with a seven-yard scoring pass that put the game out of reach. Joe threw only six passes, but completed four for 60 yards and two TD's as the 49ers won, 37–27.

Walsh later admitted that the repeated repairs of the amplifier had been a trick. "I was trying to prepare Joe to be our starting quarterback," the coach said, "so I put him in certain situations or against certain teams to give him a taste of success. Then I'd pull him back. It was a three-year project."

Beginning in mid-October, Montana started three straight games, then didn't get another start for four more weeks. But he made the most of that next opportunity.

Against New Orleans on December 7, Joe began the second half with his team behind, 35–7. He proceeded to direct four long touchdown drives totaling 331 yards, and the 49ers finally tied the game on Lenvil Elliott's seven-yard run with 1:35 left. Then Montana engineered a 55-yard drive in overtime that set up Ray Wersching's field goal, capping a 38–35 victory. It was the greatest second-half comeback in NFL history.

"A lot of people are afraid to be in that situation," Joe said after the game. "It doesn't faze me. Maybe it's my competitiveness, but I'm just as relaxed in that situation as when I'm not. I've always been competitive, whether it was throwing rocks as a kid or playing in the NFL."

Or playing golf, a sport that he made time for, no matter how busy his schedule. One morning in July 1981, Joe and his girlfriend, Cass Castillo, went out and played 18 holes. That afternoon they were married. "Joe didn't see any reason to waste the morning," said the new Mrs. Montana. They settled down on a farm south of San Francisco with their two Arabian horses and two dachshunds, Broadway (named after Joe Namath) and Bosley (after the *Charlie's Angels* character).

Then came the 1981 season—and the third year—of Bill Walsh's quarterback-development project. DeBerg had been traded to Denver, and Montana had the job to himself.

The 49ers got off to a slow start, losing two of their first three games as Joe was sacked five times by Detroit and threw an interception that Atlanta's Tom Pridemore returned 101 yards for a game-turning touchdown.

But after that the 49ers jelled quickly. The offensive line began to control the line of scrimmage, giving Joe a lot of time to throw. The receivers did a better job of getting open. And the defense was vastly improved. The 49ers routed Dallas in October, 45–14. Montana rescued them from defeat against Pittsburgh and Los Angeles, and they won 12 of their last 13 games to finish at 13-3—the best record in the NFL.

Montana passed for 304 yards and two TD's to beat the New York Giants in the playoff opener, and the 49ers were in the National Football Conference (NFC) championship game against Dallas.

But despite the October blowout, the 49ers were underdogs in the game at Candlestick Park. And Cowboy defensive end Too Tall Jones said he didn't respect the San Francisco team.

In the second quarter of the championship game, Jones had Montana cornered. Suddenly Joe faked as if to run around the big Cowboy, then stepped up and quickly drilled a 38-yard completion up the middle to Dwight Clark. He turned to Jones, fixed him with a stare, as if to say, "Respect that."

But with less than five minutes left, the 49ers trailed, 27–21, and were way back on their own 11. With two minutes left, they had advanced to midfield. "Most quarterbacks start to lose control right about here," Bill Walsh would say later. But not Joe Montana. In three plays he had moved the ball to a first down at the 13—only to miss an open receiver in the end zone.

Montana was shaken, but he didn't let it show. He sent Elliott around left end to the six. Third and three. After a time-out Joe dropped back to pass. There were 58 seconds left. His primary target, Freddie Solomon, was covered. Dwight Clark stationed himself at the back of the end zone, then began to slide in the direction Montana was running. Larry Bethea and Too Tall Jones were also running—right at Montana. Joe pumped the ball once, and the two big defensive linemen rose. As they started to come down, Montana threw—off the wrong foot. Clark leaped and caught the ball, just managing to keep his feet inbounds. Wersching's extra point made it 28–27, and when the Cowboys fumbled on the next series, the 49ers were in the Super Bowl.

On January 24, 1982, the temperature hovered around zero and the roads to the Silverdome in Pontiac, Michigan, were icy. The 49ers were caught in a huge traffic jam on their way to the game. But once the game began, they quickly made up for lost time, taking advantage of Cincinnati Bengal mistakes to take a 20–0 halftime lead. Montana dove a yard for one touchdown and passed to fullback Earl Cooper for another.

It seemed as if Cincinnati quarterback Kenny

Anderson, who had been coached at one time by Bill Walsh, was doing his best Joe Montana imitation. He drove the Bengals to two touchdowns, cutting the deficit to 20–14.

Ray Wersching's third and fourth field goals of the game gave the 49ers a comfortable edge, but Anderson refused to quit. He completed six passes in a row, the last a three-yarder to Dan Ross in the end zone. Now the Bengals were within five points, 26–21, with 15 seconds left.

But it was too late for Cincinnati. Dwight Clark recovered an onside kick and the 49ers were Super Bowl champions.

And they didn't even need a final miracle from the Comeback Kid. Joe Montana had avoided that necessity with his play in the first half, and he was voted MVP of Super Bowl XVI.

7

TERRY BRADSHAW
Super Steeler

It looked as if the underdog Los Angeles Rams would pull an upset before a crowd of 103,985 at Super Bowl XIV in Pasadena's Rose Bowl stadium.

Going into the fourth quarter on January 20, 1980, the Rams were leading the Pittsburgh Steelers, 19–17, and Steeler quarterback Terry Bradshaw felt the tension mounting all around him.

A relatively young man of 31, Bradshaw was a bruised and battered veteran of 10 years in the pro football wars. No matter how well he performed, Bradshaw continually had to put up with those who questioned his intelligence.

Yet Bradshaw, strong and agile at 6-foot-3, 210 pounds, was smart enough to help make the Steelers the most successful football team of the 1970s. He brought an inner strength to his athletic physique. He was a deeply religious man with a belief in his natural abilities. "I guess I can force myself to be smart when necessary," he repeatedly said to his critics.

Now the clock was ticking away in the Super Bowl and Bradshaw was faced with his latest challenge: how to overcome a Ram team that had taken the lead three times behind quarterback Vince Ferragamo.

With the calm authority of a proven leader, Bradshaw took the ball from the center on third down and eight at his own 27-yard line. He side-stepped the onrushing tacklers and threw to wide receiver John Stallworth, who raced home with a 73-yard touchdown that gave Pittsburgh a 24–19 lead.

With less than five minutes remaining, Bradshaw completed a 45-yard pass to Stallworth. Five plays later Franco Harris smashed over from the one to give the Steelers a 31–19 victory.

Bradshaw completed 14 of 21 passes for 309 yards and two touchdowns. For the second year in a row he was Most Valuable Player of the Super Bowl.

For all the success he enjoyed, Bradshaw's career truly had a bittersweet flavor. He was

Super Bowl XIII marked another great day for Pittsburgh's Terry Bradshaw.

still aware that some people tended to make fun of him because of his homey, wholesome attitude. His gee-whiz, aw-shucks, country-boy mannerisms helped create an image of a Li'l Abner in shoulder pads, and even Bradshaw said of himself, "I was pretty much straight— what would be classified today as a square human being."

True, the violent world of a pro football player was far removed from the peaceful life that Terry had experienced as a boy in Woodlawn, a quiet suburb of Shreveport, Louisiana.

When he was just a child, growing up in a closely knit Baptist family, his mother, Novis, took him to revival meetings. Religion had such a strong influence on Terry's life that at one time he considered becoming a minister. But sports were an equally important part of his childhood, and once Terry became aware of his extraordinary athletic skills, he decided he was meant to pursue a football career.

Although Terry described himself as "a momma's boy," he still managed to get into a lot of mischief and had to be disciplined for such things as stealing watermelons.

When he wasn't getting into trouble, Terry liked to play ball—"any kind of ball." And he loved doing the things country boys have always done—fishing, playing games barefooted in the pasture, and getting together with all his family for big cookouts. He looked forward to those plates piled high with fried chicken, sweet potatoes, corn on the cob, black-eyed peas, and home-baked pies.

Although in those carefree days Terry was an outgoing, happy-go-lucky kid, as he grew older he became more withdrawn and almost shy. This occurred because the more famous he became and the more criticism he read about himself, the more unsure he became of his abilities.

Terry was born on September 2, 1948, in Shreveport. He was a local hero at Woodlawn High School, where he not only was the star quarterback but threw the javelin 245 feet, a record distance for a U.S. schoolboy.

It was during his high-school days that Terry first began to feel something special about himself, a certain inner instinct that he had the ability to succeed in football if he was willing to pay the price with countless hours of hard work.

"Inside of me I always felt different," he recalled. "I wanted to be somebody. I wanted to be good."

And so Terry would throw a football for hours and hours into buckets he set up in his backyard.

By the time he entered Louisiana Tech in Ruston, Louisiana, 75 miles east of his home, Bradshaw was an accomplished quarterback with a cannon arm. He broke all the school passing and total offense records, connecting on 462 of 879 passes, a completion rate of 52.5 percent, for 7,149 yards and 42 touchdowns.

With no opportunity at Louisiana Tech to prove himself against the better collegiate players (because Louisiana Tech didn't play the major colleges), Bradshaw didn't attain national recognition until the 1969 Senior Bowl game in Mobile, Alabama. He completed 17 of 31 passes for 267 yards and two touchdowns, and was chosen the game's Most Valuable Player.

In the 1970 college draft the Pittsburgh Steelers had the number 1 choice after winning only one of 14 games the previous year. With little hesitation they selected Bradshaw, marking the first time a small-college player was the first pick in the draft.

Bradshaw reported to training camp as the number 3 quarterback behind Kent Nix and Terry Hanratty, but he was elevated to the starter's role in the first exhibition game. The Steelers had won only three games in the previous two years, and in 1970 they turned in a record of 5-9—better, but no reason to cheer.

When it was time to go home at the end of the year, Terry was ready to give up the game for good. In one game he had been so nervous that he had thrown up. He admitted that he had choked on other occasions because he wanted to win so desperately.

"The way I felt," he said, "I didn't know if I wanted to play football anymore."

Most of Bradshaw's troubles resulted not from his lack of ability on the field, but from his inability to adjust off the field. Until he went to Pittsburgh, he had hardly seen a big city except for New Orleans, and he wasn't prepared for all the attention that comes with being a number 1 draft choice.

And then there were the snickers, from teammates and fans alike, implying that Bradshaw wasn't smart enough to control a high-powered NFL offense. To Bradshaw, though, it was simply a matter of people not being able to accept his down-home mannerisms.

"I stood for Mom and apple pie and God bless America," he said. "I was too good to be true. I'm sure it made a lot of people turn off."

To be fair, though, it is estimated that a quarterback requires as many as five years to mature in pro ball, and it is rare that a rookie is thrown into a starter's role as Bradshaw was.

In his second year, 1971, Bradshaw started all but one game, and his numbers improved markedly with 203 completions for 2,259 yards and 13 touchdowns. The Steelers won six games for their best record in eight years.

In 1972 the Steelers turned in an 11-3 record to win their first division championship in their 39-year history.

Even at this point there were a lot of frustrations for Bradshaw. In 1973 he missed half a season because of a shoulder separation, and at the beginning of the next season he lost the starting job to Joe Gilliam, who was looked on as a better prospect.

But the turning point for Bradshaw and the Steelers came late in 1975 against Houston. Coach Chuck Noll told him, "You're my quarterback."

Bradshaw took over, and Pittsburgh won its final two games of the regular season. Then the Steelers swept through the playoffs and beat Minnesota, 16–6, in Super Bowl IX. Bradshaw's pass to Larry Brown accounted for the clinching touchdown.

It was quite a turnabout for Bradshaw. His teammate Mean Joe Greene summed it up well when he said of Bradshaw, "It was as if he had hit rock bottom right before our eyes and then pulled himself back up without anybody having to give him a hand."

Franco Harris added, "When Terry matured, we matured too. Some people find success right away, others struggle. He struggled, and we struggled with him."

For the next few years the Steelers, with Bradshaw calling the signals, continued one of the finest dynasties ever seen in the NFL.

The Steelers won the Super Bowl again in 1975, with Bradshaw throwing two TD passes, including a 64-yarder to Lynn Swann, in a 21–17 victory over Dallas.

Bradshaw enjoyed his best season in 1978 when he led the AFC in passing. He completed 56.3 percent of his passes for 2,915 yards and 28 touchdowns as Pittsburgh turned in a 14-2 regular-season record.

In the playoffs Bradshaw threw for another 790 yards and eight TD's, four of those touchdown passes coming in a 35–31 victory over Dallas in Super Bowl XIII. Bradshaw was voted the game's MVP, an honor he would repeat the following year in the Super Bowl victory over Los Angeles.

Bradshaw's fame and winning personality brought him opportunities to break into show business. He played a brawler in the Burt Reynolds movie *Hooper,* appeared in television commercials, and performed as a country-western singer.

But even after all the success he achieved, Bradshaw continued to mature and improve as a quarterback. It seems virtually certain that he will rank among the top 10 of all time in the four major passing categories—yardage, passes attempted, completions, and touchdown passes.

Off the field Bradshaw enjoys most the times when he can relax on his 400-acre horse and cattle ranch in Grand Cane, Louisiana.

There is always a touch of modesty when he talks about his accomplishments, always insisting that he was never the best, even of his own era.

"I've been a lucky quarterback," Bradshaw says. "I came along at the right time and joined a team of giants. I'm a product of my team. I was a good quarterback because I played on a great football team."

8

BOB GRIESE
Dolphin Flipper

As the Miami Dolphins' charter flight zoomed south from New Jersey, Bob Griese walked slowly down the aisle. The smallish quarterback suddenly stopped and began to touch a newsman's face.

"I can't see you, but I think I recognize your voice," Griese deadpanned, bringing a roar of laughter from those seated nearby. Earlier that day—September 11, 1977—Griese had become the first NFL quarterback to play a full game wearing eyeglasses. He had completed 13 of 18 passes for 208 yards and two touchdowns in Miami's 27–21 exhibition-game victory over the New York Giants.

The normally serious quarterback could afford to be humorous after such a performance, but things hadn't been so funny a year earlier when he was in an exhibition game against the Houston Oilers. As he stood over center, scanning the Oilers' defense, he saw Bob Brazile, the menacing linebacker, and next to him . . . another Bob Brazile! Griese remembered thinking: "Either they're doing something illegal, or there's something wrong with my eyes." Indeed, he was seeing double.

After that 1976 season, which saw the Dolphins slip to a 6-8 record—their worst in years—Griese had gone to Dr. Dave Sime for his annual eye exam. Sime, a former Olympic sprinter, determined that Griese was suffering from amblyopia—lazy eye—and prescribed glasses.

Griese decided to wear glasses off the field and try contact lenses on it. Few players wear glasses while playing because the glasses could break and cause injury. He wore the contacts in an exhibition game against New Orleans prior to the 1977 season but was forced to leave in the first quarter when he experienced dizziness and blurred vision. Determined to try another experiment, Griese asked coach Don Shula to let him play the fourth quarter—wearing glasses. He completed four of eight passes and, encouraged by his improved vision, wore

Bob Griese's vision and performance as a Miami Dolphin changed dramatically when he decided to wear glasses.

glasses again the following week in that memorable exhibition game against the Giants.

He went on to make the 1977 season his finest as a pro, leading the Dolphins to a 10-4 record. His 22 touchdown passes were a career high, and he threw for 2,252 yards.

Bob Griese was considered "the thinking-man's quarterback," noted for his intelligence in reading defenses and calling plays. And he was a high-percentage passer, preferring the low-risk pass to the long-range bomb.

But when he received the Maxwell Club's award as American Football Conference Player of the Year that December, the Dolphin quarterback delivered a bombshell: he revealed that he had played for years while legally blind in one eye!

Griese explained that he had always looked out of his left eye, and had no problem until his right eye started getting stronger. That brought it more into play with the left, causing a focusing difficulty.

He also admitted that the problem could have been discovered and corrected when he was young if he had not cheated on a school vision test.

In grammar school back home in Evansville, Indiana, young Bob Griese had known he couldn't read the columns of numbers on the eye chart with his right eye. But when the school nurse had turned her back to read the chart, he had moved the card over and read with both eyes. Although both his parents had begun to wear glasses in their early twenties, Bob was determined not to. Glasses were for sissies, he thought.

And young Bob, who was born in Evansville on February 3, 1945, was no sissy. He spent most of his free time playing sports. Baseball was his favorite, then basketball. Football was a poor third. In fact, he didn't play organized football until he was a freshman at Rex Mundi High School.

The football coach knew about Griese's arm from baseball and asked him to try out at quarterback.

"He told me to run 27 Paula," Griese would recall years later. "I got in the huddle and shouted '27 Paula!' Everybody laughed. I turned around and the coach was standing over me, shouting 'Powuh! Powuh!' He had a big New England accent."

Griese's father had died when Bob was 10, and his mother had the difficult task of raising two sons and a daughter by herself. When Bob was a sophomore in high school, his brother was a senior at a different Catholic school, and this posed a problem for their mother when the two schools met in football. Bob was the quarterback for his team; his brother was the defensive middle guard, playing right over center. Before one such game the local paper did an article on Mrs. Griese, trying to find out who she would be cheering for. She solved the problem by sitting on the 50-yard line, holding a pompon from each school, and cheering for both teams.

Although he excelled in football at Rex Mundi, Bob's main sport remained baseball. By the time he was 18, the major-league scouts were in hot pursuit. After the American Legion World Series in New Hampshire, the Baltimore Orioles offered him a contract.

Bob gave it a lot of thought, then decided he didn't want to risk not making it to the major leagues and getting "lost forever in the minor leagues." He felt he could always play baseball in college. As it turned out, he never did.

He did play basketball his first two years at Purdue, starting at guard as a sophomore. His progress in football wasn't as rapid, because he was basically self-taught and had picked up "some bad habits" in high school. One of these was throwing three-quarters sidearm, as he had done in baseball. But Purdue backfield coach

Bob Demoss taught him the conventional style, and Griese's career blossomed. He became a starter during his sophomore year, but had just a fair season. The best was yet to come.

Griese gazed at the crowd packed into Purdue's stadium on a beautiful September day in 1965—it was the largest ever to attend a football game in the state of Indiana. It was early in Bob's junior year, and the Boilermakers were about to play intrastate rival Notre Dame, the number 1 team in the nation.

Three years earlier Griese had considered attending Notre Dame. He had wanted to stay close to home and was planning a visit to the South Bend campus. Then an alumnus came to him and said Notre Dame was not interested in the young quarterback because he was too small (Griese barely reached 6 feet standing on tiptoes, and weighed about 170). He didn't make the visit, deciding that if they weren't interested in him, he wasn't interested in them.

Now, Griese was interested in the Notre Dame defense. As always, he analyzed it, looking for a weakness to exploit. He found one by sending out five receivers on most passing downs, keeping the Irish secondary off-balance throughout the game.

Griese threw three touchdown passes, two to tight end Jim Beirne. But the Irish kept fighting back and took a 21–18 lead on Ken Ivan's field goal with less than six minutes left in the game.

Griese wasted no time. Starting at his own 33, he moved Purdue into scoring position in just three plays—a 32-yard pass to flanker Jim Finley and completions of 13 and 19 yards to Beirne. He then handed off to halfback Gordon Tyler, who went the final three yards for the touchdown that capped a 69-second drive and gave Purdue a 25–21 upset. Bob Griese had beaten the team that didn't want him.

The rest of Griese's junior year wasn't as satisfying. Purdue had a chance at the Rose Bowl bid, but lost to a mediocre Illinois team, assuring Michigan State of a trip to Pasadena.

But the next season—1966—Purdue won the Big Ten title and earned its first-ever Rose Bowl berth. Griese achieved a first too. No other Purdue player had ever been named the Big Ten's MVP in the 43-year history of the award. He also won All-America honors for the second straight season.

On January 2, 1967, in the Rose Bowl, Griese proved he was worthy of such recognition when he showed his all-around abilities. Evading tacklers and getting the ball away when it appeared he would be trapped for a loss, he completed 10 of 18 passes for 139 yards, kicked two extra points, and did the punting as Purdue scored a 14–13 victory over the University of Southern California.

A few days later triumph almost turned into tragedy for Griese and George Catavolos, a defensive back who had also starred in the Rose Bowl game. They were in Hawaii to play in the Hula Bowl all-star game and rented a Jeep to do some sightseeing. Finding an inviting beach, they decided to go swimming. Catavolos got caught in an undertow and was carried out into the ocean. Griese went after him. The two friends tired as they struggled to shore and might have drowned if a Hawaiian hadn't come to the rescue.

Returning home, Griese told a friend he was going to get married soon. "That was a close call," he said, "and I'm not going to take any more chances of missing anything in life." So he proposed to his college sweetheart, Judi, whom he married later in the year.

In spring 1967 Joe Thomas, personnel director of the Miami Dolphins, was prepared to take a chance in the NFL draft, but he hoped he wouldn't have to. Thomas wanted to draft Bob Griese in the first round. The Dolphins had finished last in 1966, their first year in the AFL, and wanted a quarterback to lead them out of the wilderness.

Many Florida fans were hoping they would get Steve Spurrier, the Heisman Trophy winner from the University of Florida. Joe Thomas disagreed. "Griese is much quicker," Thomas told his associates, "and he's a much better runner. The only other difference between them is the local appeal Spurrier would have." But this was no small consideration for a second-year team struggling to hike its home attendance above 30,000 a game.

That year's draft was the first held jointly by the AFL and NFL. The Dolphins were to pick fourth, behind Baltimore, Minnesota, and Atlanta. After the Colts and the Vikings made their selections, Joe Thomas got the break he was looking for. The Falcons traded their pick to San Francisco for three players. When the 49ers announced they had selected "Steve Spurrier, quarterback, University of Florida," Thomas let out a whoop that could be heard all the way from Miami to draft headquarters in New York. The Dolphins wasted no time in drafting their man—Bob Griese.

Griese was happy too. He would be able to play in warm weather and get a chance to start earlier than a young quarterback with an established team. He didn't realize how soon that chance would come.

Four minutes into the Dolphins' 1967 home opener against the Denver Broncos, Griese stood on the sideline at the Orange Bowl, watching as a stretcher was carried out onto the field. John Stofa, the Dolphins' starting quarterback, lay on the turf with a broken ankle.

Coach George Wilson yelled to Griese to warm up, then came over to discuss how to move the ball—which was on the Miami three—into position for Larry Seiple to punt it away.

But Wilson let the young quarterback call his own plays. Griese turned to his running backs, and they moved the ball far enough to give Seiple ample kicking room. The success of this first series increased Griese's confidence. So did his first pass completion and his first touchdown pass. The Dolphins won, and Griese had established himself as the Dolphins' quarterback.

There would be few victories the next few years, but after the 1969 season, owner Joe Robbie brought in coach Don Shula, who surrounded Griese with a strong supporting cast.

Griese quickly became an on-field extension of his coach. Both were serious-minded and thorough, and they thought alike. The Dolphins gained their first playoff berth in Shula's initial season, 1970. The next year they beat Kansas City in a memorable double-overtime game on Christmas Day to reach the AFC championship game. Then they beat Baltimore to reach the Super Bowl against the Dallas Cowboys.

But Griese had a frustrating time in the Super Bowl on January 16, 1972, when Dallas' Doomsday Defense chased him all over New Orleans' Tulane Stadium—throwing him for a 29-yard loss on one play—and the Cowboys crushed the Dolphins, 24–3.

Griese was determined to do better in the 1972 season and he led the Dolphins to victories in their first four games. Then, early in the fifth game, San Diego's Ron East hit him as he was about to pass. Broken ankle.

Earl Morrall, Griese's 39-year-old backup, stepped in and led the Dolphins to 11 straight victories. But the old man faltered in the AFC championship game, and Griese started the second half with Pittsburgh leading the Dolphins, 10–7.

Although he hadn't played since his injury— except for a brief tuneup in the final regular-season game—Griese wasted no time making his presence felt. Hearing a few ideas being mumbled in the huddle, he snapped "Shut up" and called the play. He took charge of the game just as quickly, directing an 80-yard scoring drive that gave the Dolphins the lead for good. They won, 21–10, and now only Washington stood in the way of a perfect season.

In the two weeks before Super Bowl VII, Griese, Shula, and the rest of the coaching staff studied the Redskins intensively. So when Griese took the field at the Los Angeles Coliseum, he felt he knew what the Dolphins could do and when they could do it.

And he proceeded to do pretty much as he wanted, completing six of six passes—including a 28-yard scoring strike to Howard Twilley—as Miami took a 14–0 halftime lead. The defense did the rest, shutting off the Redskins and allowing Griese to play conservatively in the second half. Miami won, 14–7, and the "perfect quarterback" had completed the only perfect season in NFL history—17 victories without a defeat.

Griese remained healthy the next season and led the Dolphins into an unprecedented third straight Super Bowl, this time against Minnesota. Relying mainly on the running of Larry Csonka, Miami took a 17–0 halftime lead and breezed to a 24–7 victory.

Griese never got to another Super Bowl, but the Dolphins remained contenders for the rest of the 1970s. In a game against Baltimore in 1980, he became the fourteenth passer to join the NFL's exclusive 25,000-yard club. That same day he suffered a shoulder injury that forced his retirement after 14 seasons. After one year as an assistant coach, Griese embarked on a new career in 1982—as an analyst on NBC-TV's coverage of NFL games.

9

FRAN TARKENTON
The Viking Scrambler

As a youngster, Fran Tarkenton enjoyed playing games that he invented. There was one Fran especially liked. He would use pictures of college and professional football players and form two teams. Then he would line up the players by position and play an imaginary game. Sammy Baugh, the great Washington Redskin quarterback in the 1940s, was one of Fran's favorites. During these games Fran imagined he was a quarterback too.

Tarkenton was always using his head—a useful quality for someone who was not particularly big and strong. His father was a Methodist preacher who was very strict. No one smoked, drank alcohol, or cursed in the Tarkenton home. Everyone went to church regularly.

But that did not mean that Fran wasn't allowed to play football. The Tarkentons moved

from Richmond, Virginia, where Fran was born on February 3, 1940, to Washington, D.C. Later they moved to Athens, Georgia, where at the age of 11 Fran tried out for his elementary school team. Athens is the site of the University of Georgia, deep in the heart of football country. Just the kind of place where a new Sammy Baugh could get a start.

It seemed only natural that Fran try out for quarterback at Athens High School. Despite being small for his age, he became a starter when he was in ninth grade. Two years later, as a junior, Fran led Athens to an unbeaten season and a chance to win the state title against Valdosta.

Not only was he the quarterback, but Fran ran back kickoffs too. And on the opening kickoff of the title game, he ran it back for a touchdown. Before his teammates could celebrate, however, they noticed that a penalty flag had been thrown. The touchdown did not count.

So Fran simply ran back the next kickoff for a touchdown. This time there were no penalty flags. Athens went on to win the state title. Afterward Fran Tarkenton revealed that he had

Minnesota's Fran Tarkenton gets caught in a scramble against Miami in Super Bowl VIII.

played the entire season with a separated shoulder.

Unfortunately he and his team had a disappointing season in his senior year. His confidence was shattered. He enrolled at Georgia, but he wondered whether he would even make the freshman team.

Because Athens was his home, Fran felt comfortable in college when many of his fellow freshmen were homesick. His confidence on the football field was restored by freshman coach Quinton Lumpkin. Although the freshmen played only three games, Fran was outstanding and showed head coach Wally Butts he was ready to start for the upperclassmen too.

In 1958, Fran's sophomore year, he began the season as the third-string quarterback. He would have to wait his turn, it seemed. In the opening game against Texas, Georgia was losing in the third quarter, 7–0, and the offense had sputtered to a stop. While coach Butts watched, frustrated, from the sideline, Fran walked over to him and pleaded, "Let me go in. I can move the team."

Butts said nothing. Then Georgia regained possession, and this time Fran Tarkenton did not ask to play again. He just ran onto the field, trying not to hear Butts yelling at him to get off.

It was too late for Butts to stop him. Tarkenton then moved Georgia 95 yards to a touchdown. After the two-point conversion his team led, 8–7.

Wally Butts was angry, though. He had not given Tarkenton permission to play. Fran knew he should not have taken matters into his own hands. When Georgia got the football again, Fran was back on the bench. The Bulldogs lost that game, but a young man had learned a valuable lesson. He could not expect to become a leader unless he too was willing to listen to directions.

Fran had too much talent and intelligence to stay on the bench for long. By the middle of that 1958 season he was the starting quarterback. The next year he became an All-Southeast Conference selection and led Georgia to a 14–0 victory over Missouri in the Orange Bowl. Life was wonderful off the field as well. Fran met a girl named Elaine at a party on campus. She was a majorette in the band. "I just found the right girl," he told a friend. She would soon become Mrs. Tarkenton.

Before the start of the 1960 season, Fran's senior year, he was picked as an All-American. Teams in the NFL had their eye on him. People were no longer saying that he was too small to be a professional quarterback. He was 6-foot-1 and weighed 190 pounds.

But smart, good quarterbacks need help too. In his last year at Georgia, Tarkenton didn't get much help. Nor was it the best season he had ever had. Georgia slipped to a 6-4 record. Now the scouts weren't so sure. The Minnesota Vikings, a first-year team in the NFL, picked Fran in the third round of the draft. "I don't think coach Butts thinks I can make it in the pros," Fran said. "I'm going to prove them all wrong."

The Vikings were a collection of rookies, free agents, and veterans not wanted by other teams. Norm Van Brocklin, who had been an excellent quarterback in his day, was the coach. He chose George Shaw, a veteran who had taken plenty of poundings, as his first-string signal caller. "Look, Fran," Van Brocklin told the rookie, "we want to bring you along slowly."

On the Tuesday before the opening game of the 1961 season, though, Van Brocklin was wavering. "I think I'll start you," he told Tarkenton. By Friday he had changed his mind again. It didn't matter, though. Fran Tarkenton was prepared.

George Shaw started the first game the Vikings ever played. But he didn't last for long. Early in the first quarter Fran Tarkenton, num-

ber 10, trotted onto the field to face the fero-
cious Chicago Bears' defense. Minnesota was
playing at home, and the Viking fans feared the
rookie would get his lumps.

Instead he led the Vikings to an amazing
37–13 victory. Fran was dazzling as he artfully
dodged the Bears' defensive front four all afternoon. Just when it looked as if he would be
tackled, he would squirm out of the grasp of the
defense. A quarterback is expected to stay in
the protective pocket formed by his blockers,
but Tarkenton repeatedly left the pocket and
frustrated the Bears.

It was that way all season as Tarkenton scampered here and scampered there, confusing his
opponents with a mixture of passes and runs.
He finished eighth in the NFL in passing and
threw 18 touchdown passes. And because of his
unique running ability, he rushed for 308 yards
and five touchdowns. The Vikings won only
three games, but they were an exciting team
that gained respect from their competitors.

Unfortunately the Vikings did not improve in
1962. Their record, in fact, was 2-11-1, worse
than in their first year. And the fans who had
warmed to the gutsy little quarterback from
Georgia during the previous cold Minnesota
winter were now turning against Tarkenton.

The young man could not quite understand it.

There was one game in which the fans began to chant for John McCormick, Fran's understudy. Norm Van Brocklin sent in McCormick. As Tarkenton walked to the sidelines, he felt embarrassed and alone. Hugh McElhenny, the veteran running back, put his arm around Fran and consoled him. "You've made it now, kid," he said. "They've booed you and you've been replaced. You're an NFL quarterback."

It was a year of tough breaks for Tarkenton. In a game against Baltimore he was knocked unconscious by defensive back Wendell Harris. It took a while for Fran to regain his senses.

That did not stop Tarkenton from running with the ball, however. He continued to perplex the opposition with his unorthodox style. In the 1963 season he led the Vikings to only five victories. But in 1964 the team was maturing and seemed ready to challenge Baltimore and Green Bay for the Western Conference title.

The Vikings were playing the Packers, and Tarkenton already had begun to be called The Scrambler. Late in the game the Vikings trailed, 23–21, and the situation seemed hopeless. There was less than a minute left, fourth down and 22 yards to go. In the huddle, Tarkenton told his teammates: "We've got to do something drastic. All you receivers run downfield twenty-five yards. I'll scramble around until I find one of you open."

It was the first time Tarkenton had actually called a scramble. And it worked. He ran around and around until he threw a desperation pass that Gordie Smith caught for a first down in Green Bay territory. Shortly afterward Fred Cox kicked a field goal to give Minnesota a 24–23 victory. The Vikings won eight games that season and tied for second in the conference.

Now the Vikings were contenders. The experts picked them to win the Western title. But they finished only 7-7 in 1965, and the first hints of a falling out between Van Brocklin and Tarkenton began to surface.

The coach was an old-fashioned type who had never gotten accustomed to Tarkenton's scrambling. But as long as the Vikings won, Van Brocklin would not try to make his quarterback change. For his part, Fran was headstrong and stubborn. He felt he knew how to run the offense better than his coach.

In 1966 the Vikings landed with a thud. They won only four games. Van Brocklin threatened to quit and Tarkenton asked to be traded. The two tried to settle their differences and even hugged and vowed to make the Vikings champions. But during the off-season Tarkenton realized this was wishful thinking.

So Fran wrote a letter to the Vikings' board of directors requesting a trade. And they accommodated him. He was traded to the New York Giants for three number 1 draft choices. He was going to the big city.

Could the son of a preacher live the fast life in New York? Fran Tarkenton could. With his easy manner and pleasant personality, he adjusted easily. New York suited him fine. He went to the fancy restaurants, he dressed in the latest styles, and he compared notes with Joe Namath, the playboy quarterback of the New York Jets.

On the field, however, nothing had changed. The Giants had won only one game in 1966 and their prospects were not good. But with Tarkenton at quarterback, they won seven games in 1967 and rekindled the fans' hopes. They won seven games again the following year before dropping to a 6-8 record in 1969. Still disappointing for a team with a great past, but at least Tarkenton had made the Giants respectable again.

The high point of Tarkenton's New York experience came in 1970, when he led the Giants to their best season in seven years. On the final Sunday they fought for a playoff berth in a game against the Rams.

The Giants lost, however, and their 9-5 record seemed like a mirage. "Without Fran," said defensive end Fred Dryer, "I don't think we would have won any games."

When the Giants fell to 4-10 in 1971, Tarkenton sensed that he had outlived his usefulness in New York. He was 32 years old and had never played for a legitimate contender. Once again he was at odds with management, this time disagreeing with Giants coach Alex Webster. In a trade that made both sides happy, Tarkenton was sent back to the Vikings.

But these weren't the old Vikings. The new team had won four division titles in a row. Coach Bud Grant felt that a veteran quarterback like Tarkenton was the key to winning the Super Bowl. Fran was thrilled.

"To be able to play on a team like this is fun," he told friends. "I don't care how much money you're making; if you don't win, the game is a drag."

For Tarkenton, however, there would be still another test of his will and confidence. In 1972 the best the Vikings could do was a 7-7 record. Fran kept moving up on the all-time list of quarterbacks, but he had not yet been in the playoffs.

The years of frustration ended in 1973. The Vikings finished with a 12-2 record and won the Central Division title in the National Conference. They defeated Washington and Dallas in the playoffs to advance to Super Bowl VIII. Fran Tarkenton was on top of the world.

Now no one was making fun of scrambling quarterbacks. In fact, many teams began to draft quarterbacks who could run as well as pass. "People looked down on scrambling quarterbacks when I broke in," Fran said, "but now those who can't scramble are at a disadvantage."

Miami defeated the Vikings, 24–7, in the Super Bowl, but Tarkenton had gotten a taste of the playoffs and promised to be back. He and the Vikings returned the next year to face the Pittsburgh Steelers in Super Bowl IX. Once again a magnificent season was spoiled when the powerful Steelers won, 16–6. This time Tarkenton was more disappointed. "I want to win a championship desperately," he said. "It's probably what I want more than anything in the world. But if I don't, I won't kill myself."

In 1975 Tarkenton again led the Vikings to a 12-2 record and was voted Most Valuable Player in the NFL.

But the Vikings were beaten early in the playoffs by Dallas. In 1976 their amazing string of success continued as Tarkenton, now a mature pro of 36, led his team to Super Bowl XI against the Oakland Raiders. People seemed to sense that Fran would not have many more opportunities to win his championship.

He seemed more on edge than usual during Super Bowl Week in Los Angeles. This was the Vikings' fourth appearance in the championship game—their third with Fran. Even though they had made it to the Super Bowl three times, the Vikings were called losers because they had not won.

This time the Vikings promised it would be different. "This team has a new dimension," said coach Grant. "Emotion."

Late in the opening quarter, Minnesota's Fred McNeil did something no other team had done before—he blocked one of Ray Guy's punts. It put the ball on the Oakland 3-yard line. A Minnesota touchdown would put the Vikings ahead for the first time in a Super Bowl game.

But Brent McClanahan fumbled and Oakland then drove 90 yards to set up a field goal by Errol Mann.

From there the Raiders rolled up a 16–0 lead before Tarkenton got off a touchdown pass to Sammy White. It was not enough to change the outcome. Oakland won the game handily, 32–14.

In both 1977 and 1978 the Vikings barely squeezed into the playoffs and were eliminated before getting to the Super Bowl. When 1979 approached, Tarkenton had made up his mind that it was his final season—championship or no championship.

"I've played this game since I was eleven years old," he said. "I don't want to hang around for a paycheck. You wake up and you're thirty-nine and you know it's time to move on."

Football was a game for younger men. Tarkenton did not want to become an understudy for a promising newcomer. The Vikings finished 7-9 in 1979, but once again, it was not because Fran had failed. During the year he tutored Tommy Kramer, who became his successor, but Fran never lost his job to him.

When the season ended, he formally announced his retirement. He went on to manage his successful business ventures in his hometown of Atlanta and to become a television football announcer and co-host of the series *That's Incredible*.

In 18 years he had played more games (257) at his position than anyone else. He had surpassed legends like Johnny Unitas and Sammy

Baugh—his boyhood hero—to become the all-time leader in completions, yardage gained, and touchdown passes. He never won a championship, but Viking coach Bud Grant said, "He is the greatest quarterback ever to play this game."

10

JOHNNY UNITAS
The Colt from Pittsburgh

Yankee Stadium had become strangely quiet. More than 60,000 fans sat huddled in warm clothing and blankets, fighting off the cold of a late Sunday afternoon in December 1958. They were hoping for a miracle—a fumble, perhaps. But on the field the Baltimore Colts felt invigorated by the chill. They were warmed by the knowledge that a victory against the New York Giants in the NFL championship game was only one yard away. And they were in the capable hands of a young, daring quarterback named Johnny Unitas.

Starting with less than two minutes to play in regulation time, Unitas had guided the Colts on an 86-yard drive that resulted in a 20-yard field goal by Steve Myrha that tied the score, 17–17, and sent the game into sudden-death overtime.

Johnny Unitas' mighty arm made him a long-time favorite in Baltimore and throughout the nation.

Now the lanky quarterback had brought the Colts to within three feet of the title by completing a gambling seven-yard pass to tight end Jim Mutscheller, to the amazement of everyone but his teammates.

Baltimore coach Weeb Ewbank stood on the sidelines, not bothering to send in a play. He had confidence in Unitas. "Sixteen-power," the quarterback said in the huddle. The play was designed for Alan (The Horse) Ameche, the big, bruising fullback. As the crowd watched silently, Unitas took the snap and handed off to Ameche. The fullback crashed into the end zone with little resistance and the Baltimore Colts were champions, 23–17. A quarterback who was playing in only his third year had led his team to victory in what many would call "the greatest game ever played."

Johnny Unitas never dreamed he would play professional football. He was born on May 7, 1933, in Pittsburgh, one of four children of a steelworker and his wife. Life was hard for many people during the Great Depression. But it became even worse for the Unitas family when Leonard Unitas died. His son Johnny was only five years old.

Mrs. Unitas did the best she could for her

family. She ran a coal delivery business during the day and worked as a scrubwoman at night in downtown Pittsburgh. When the coal business failed, she got a job in a bakery while attending school at night. Eventually she became a bookkeeper for the city.

When Johnny was old enough, he helped out by earning 75 cents for every ton of coal he could shovel into neighborhood bins. He also played football—as a running back and receiver—at St. Justin's, a small Catholic high school. Unitas was a skinny youngster who barely weighed 145 pounds. He didn't become a quarterback until his senior year, and then it was literally by accident.

The accident occurred to the regular quarterback, who broke an ankle. The coach wanted to replace him with someone who had a strong arm. Johnny Unitas had the best arm on the team. He had an impressive season, earning All-Catholic honors in Pittsburgh. But because he had gotten such a late start and was so thin, not many colleges were interested in offering Johnny a scholarship.

He applied to Notre Dame, but his grades were not good enough. He couldn't meet the entrance exam requirements at the University of Pittsburgh. Indiana didn't even bother to answer his application. Finally Unitas was accepted at Louisville, a school whose reputation in basketball was much stronger than in football.

Johnny was the third-string quarterback as a freshman in 1951 and was almost cut from the team. But soon he began to impress his coaches with that strong right arm. And he impressed his opponents too. Even though Louisville was soundly defeated, 59–6, by powerful Tennessee, coach Bowden Wyatt of the Volunteers said Unitas was the best quarterback he had seen all year.

Although Louisville continued to lose more games than it won every season, Unitas continued to develop as an excellent passer. And despite that scrawny, six-foot, 145-pound frame, he showed he was tough too. In his senior year he suffered a hairline fracture of his ankle but missed only one game.

When his college career ended in 1954, he had broken 15 school records. He also had added some muscle and weighed 190 pounds. He seemed destined for the pros.

His college coach thought so, anyway. When Frank Camp saw how Unitas had battled against injuries and a lack of support from his teammates, the coach said, "He'll show the same courage in the pros."

Yet no one seemed too interested in Unitas. The Pittsburgh Steelers of the NFL made the hometown boy a ninth-round draft pick in 1955, but Unitas did not get a long look from the Steelers, either. He was not given an opportunity to play during the exhibition games and was cut at training camp.

Johnny was disappointed. He would not have minded had he tried and failed, but he felt he had never even been given a chance. "That's all I want," he told coach Butch Kiesling. Instead he was given $10 for the bus ride home to Pittsburgh.

Unitas was married now and his wife, Dorothy, was pregnant. Johnny was 22 years old and he had to find a job. During the week he worked on a pile-driving gang, oiling and greasing rigs. And on Saturday night he pursued his first love. Unitas was a quarterback for the Bloomfield Rams, a sandlot team. He earned $6 a game.

"It's all right," Dorothy Unitas told her husband. "I know you have to get it out of your system."

But Johnny Unitas still held on to his goal of playing in the NFL. In February 1956 Don Kellett, the general manager of the Baltimore

Colts, called to invite Unitas to camp for a try-out.

This time Johnny was unsure. He was working in construction and felt he needed the steady job because his baby was almost due. But his wife persuaded him to give pro football another chance. In May he went to the tryout and impressed coach Weeb Ewbank. He was signed to a $7,000 contract. "This is triple what I made back home playing for the Bloomfield Rams," he said jokingly. Actually it seemed like a fortune to Unitas.

George Shaw was the Colts' starting quarter-back, and Unitas was happy just to make the team as a reserve. But when Shaw was injured in the fourth game of the 1956 season, Johnny was suddenly pressed into service.

It was a game he would never forget. Unitas did not break in like a storybook hero, throwing touchdown passes to all his receivers. Instead he played like the nervous, tentative rookie that he was. Johnny fumbled three times and the Chicago Bears converted all three into touchdowns. He threw a pass directly to defensive back J. C. Caroline, who ran back the interception 59 yards for a touchdown. When Unitas entered the game, the Colts led, 21–20. By the game's end, however, the Bears had surged to a

56–21 victory. The prospects were not bright for Unitas.

But he was not discouraged. From the time his high-school coach converted him to quarterback, Johnny always had confidence in his ability to run a team. It didn't matter whether it was the high-school team or the Baltimore Colts.

After that poor performance against the Bears he said, "I'm the only quarterback they have."

Still, it was a rough season, and as the final game approached, there were rumors that Ewbank would be fired.

The final game was against the Washington Redskins, the Colts' chief rivals. The Redskins led, 17–12, with time running out when Unitas threw a long desperation pass for Jim Mutscheller. Players from both teams leaped for the ball and it bounced off the shoulder pads of Norb Hecker, the Washington safety. Mutscheller caught the deflected pass and fell into the end zone for the winning touchdown. The Colts and Unitas had saved their coach's job.

Though George Shaw returned in 1957, Unitas now was the number 1 quarterback. He was becoming a familiar sight to the Colts' fans in his blue jersey with the number 19, his high-top football shoes, and his crewcut. He was still thin for the pros but heftier than before. Unitas was 6-foot-1 and weighed close to 200 pounds.

In his first full season he led the Colts to a 7-5 record and a third-place finish in the Western Conference. In fact, until they lost their last two games, it looked as if the Colts might actually win the conference title. Unitas had an excellent year, passing for 2,550 yards and 24 touchdowns—only four TD's short of Sid Luckman's NFL record.

Then came 1958, when the Colts stormed to the top of the Western Conference by winning their first six games. The sixth was a 56–0 rout of Green Bay, but there was a price to pay. Unitas, who had already thrown three touchdown passes as the game entered the third quarter, was tackled hard while scrambling and had to be helped from the field.

The injury report looked bad. He had suffered three broken ribs and a punctured lung. The Colts' chances of winning the NFL title seemed punctured too.

But after missing only one week of practice, Unitas returned, wearing an aluminum corset with rubber padding to protect his ribs. George Shaw had taken over at quarterback, as Johnny had done for Shaw the year before, and the Colts continued to play well.

When Unitas finally started three weeks after the Packer game, he showed the Los Angeles Rams that it would be business as usual. On the first play from scrimmage he faked a short pass and threw long to Lenny Moore. The play covered 53 yards and resulted in a touchdown. The Colts went on to win, 34–7.

It was a wonderful season—the Colts finished first in the Western Conference and then beat the Giants in that dramatic overtime game at Yankee Stadium.

And 1959 was even better: Unitas led the Colts to another conference championship and a rematch with the Giants in the NFL title game.

He threw 32 touchdown passes that season, breaking the league record held by Sid Luckman. Against the Giants, he directed a fourth-quarter rally that saw the Colts overcome a 9–7 deficit to win the championship, 31–16. Baltimore and its exciting young quarterback were riding high.

But 1960 was a rude awakening. After jumping off to a 6-2 start, the Colts lost Alan Ameche, their workhorse fullback, who tore his Achilles tendon. Now they were strictly a passing team. Unitas was often brilliant, but the opposing teams knew he was going to pass. He took a beating—especially during one game against the Chicago Bears. The Colts won that day, but Unitas left the field dazed and aching all over. His face was cut and bruised.

"You don't replace a guy like Ameche," Johnny said. "Now teams can key on me."

Instead of a dynasty, the Colts had become an average team. They were exciting to watch and always threatened to win, but too much was expected of Unitas. Baltimore had disappointing seasons in 1961, 1962, and 1963, and it was the Green Bay Packers under coach Vince Lombardi who became the dominating force in the league.

Unitas took a battering. He suffered injuries to his passing arm and his knees. He disagreed openly with coach Ewbank, who wanted his quarterback to play more conservatively and reduce the risk of getting hurt. But Johnny did not know how to play it safe. "If I am going to worry about getting hurt, I'll keep the ball on the ground all day and let someone else take the criticism," he said. Ewbank was fired after the 1962 season.

Don Shula took over as coach in 1963, but it wasn't until a year later that the Colts climbed back to the top. They finished 12-2 in the Western Conference and scored a league-high 428 points. Unitas was named to the All-Pro team. But the season was spoiled for Unitas and his Colts in the championship game when the Cleveland Browns shut out Baltimore, 27–0.

Johnny Unitas would never let one game discourage him. "You have to gamble in this league," he liked to say, "or you die." He was having a magnificent season in 1965 until the twelfth game when the Bears again injured him. This time his knee required surgery, and Unitas could only watch as the Colts lost a Western Conference playoff to the Packers with halfback Tom Matte forced to take Unitas' place at quarterback.

Unitas rebounded again, although Green Bay won again in 1966. When the NFL went to divisional play in 1967, Johnny led the Colts to an 11-1-2 record in the Coastal Division. The Colts did not make the playoffs, though, because the Rams finished with the same record and scored more points in the two games between the teams.

In 1968 the Colts regained the role of NFL powerhouse as they rolled to a 13-1 record. But Johnny Unitas was a spectator. A muscle tear near his elbow ended his season during the exhibition games. It was Earl Morrall who led the Colts to the NFL title.

But then came Super Bowl III in Miami, and the Colts were big favorites to beat the New York Jets of the AFL. Joe Namath, the Jets' cocky young quarterback, led his team to perhaps the biggest upset in pro football history. Unitas came off the bench to try to rescue the Colts and led them to their only touchdown—but it was too late. The Jets won, 16–7.

In 1969 the Colts finished second in the Coastal Division. Unitas was named Player of the Decade in the NFL. The following year he took the Colts to Super Bowl V against the Dallas Cowboys, but he was injured early in the game and it was Morrall who guided the Colts to a 16–13 victory.

Johnny Unitas was 37 years old now and nearing the end of his career. There would be one more fling with success as he took the Colts to the playoffs in 1971, but he was intercepted three times by Miami in a 21–0 loss.

Unitas was benched during the 1972 season in favor of Marty Domres, a youngster who had gone to Columbia. The fans had been hard on Johnny on occasion, but on December 3, in his last game in Baltimore, they stood and gave him a three-minute ovation. "Unitas We Stand," a banner read.

Johnny wasn't ready to accept retirement,

though. Although he was linked forever to Baltimore, although the horseshoe symbol on the Colts' helmets formed a "U" as in Unitas, Johnny accepted a trade to San Diego in 1973 in order to play another season.

He was 40 years old and his knees ached. Sometimes he could hardly walk. The Chargers won only two games that year and Unitas finally retired. He had played 18 seasons, and many consider him the best quarterback who ever played. Unitas completed 2,830 of 5,186 passes for 40,239 yards and 290 touchdowns. Four times he led the league in touchdown passes. And he held the record for throwing scoring passes in 47 consecutive games.

It was quite a harvest for the skinny kid from the sandlots of Pittsburgh.

Other paperbacks in the
RANDOM HOUSE SPORTS LIBRARY

BASKETBALL'S MAGNIFICENT BIRD:
The Larry Bird Story

BORN TO HIT:
The George Brett Story

HERSCHEL WALKER:
From the Georgia Backwoods and
the Heisman Trophy to the Pros

THE MASKED MARVELS:
Baseball's Great Catchers

MIKE SCHMIDT:
Baseball's King of Swing

SPORTS TEASERS:
A Book of Games and Puzzles

STRANGE BUT TRUE BASKETBALL STORIES

STRANGE BUT TRUE FOOTBALL STORIES

SUPER BOWL SUPERSTARS:
The Most Valuable Players
in the NFL's Championship Game

TOUCHDOWN!
Football's Most Dramatic Scoring Feats

WINNERS UNDER 21:
America's Spectacular Young Sports Champions

WORLD SERIES HEROES AND GOATS:
The Men Who Made History
in America's October Classic